THE HUMANITY OF GOD

KARL BARTH

THE
HUMANITY
OF GOD

WESTMINSTER
JOHN KNOX PRESS
LOUISVILLE · KENTUCKY

Library of Congress Catalog Card Number: 60-5479

33 32 31 30 29 28 27

ISBN: 978-0-8042-0612-9

Originally published as three separate monographs in the *Theologische Studien* series by Evangelischer Verlag A. G., Zollikon-Zurich.

Evangelische Theologie im 19. Jahrhundert, translated by Thomas Wieser
Die Menschlichkeit Gottes, translated by John Newton Thomas
Das Geschenk der Freiheit, translated by Thomas Wieser

Printed in the United States of America

TRANSLATORS' PREFACE

The three essays by Karl Barth drawn together in this volume speak very well for themselves. It may be useful, however, to point out why they are being made available at this time in English.

First of all, the essays contain a concise and recent treatment of some of the central issues in Barth's theology, or for that matter in any Christian theology. This is especially true in the case of *The Humanity of God* and *The Gift of Freedom* which outline Barth's approach to Christology and to ethics respectively. Both of these areas are treated by him much more thoroughly in various parts of his *Church Dogmatics*, but the sheer length of that work may rather limit its reading audience even though it is now appearing in English. Hence it is hoped that the publication of these shorter writings will make more widely accessible some of the basic emphases in the recent and most mature form of Barth's theology.

In addition to the importance of their subject matter these essays are significant in that they reflect a certain development in Barth's thinking. The mere *fact* of this development needs to be underscored. In America and in Britain, Barth's theology is often understood and judged primarily on the basis of some of his earlier writings available in English. It is no longer possible, however, to think and speak responsibly about him if one's knowledge is limited to the earlier writings. The three essays published here illustrate in brief form both the fact and the direction of the development in Barth's thought.

The first of these essays, *Evangelical Theology in the 19th Century*, reminds us that Barth has always had tremendous respect for the past, and that he has worked out his own theology in continuous dialogue with the Christian thinkers of preceding ages. In particular, it presents a recent and concise interpretation and appraisal by him of the theology against which he and his colleagues revolted in the second decade of our century. This retrospective view provides an excellent introduction to the next essay, *The Humanity of God*, in which Barth in 1956 looks back across some forty years of his own theological work and appraises the reaction against 19th-century liberal theology in which he himself was the most distinguished leader. In undiminished appreciation of both the need and the nature of this revolt, Barth sounds the call for a new change of direction in evangelical theology, hardly, if at all, less radical than that which took place just after the First World War. With honesty and forthrightness he asserts the need for correction of the extremes to which he and his colleagues went in their early development of the *Theology of the Word*. The key to this new change he finds in a deeper understanding of Christology and its implications. In the third essay, *The Gift of Freedom*, Barth proposes an approach to evangelical ethics which proceeds from the fact that God has made man free by choosing him to be His creature, partner, and child. He opposes ethics which merely sets up rules to be applied in a given situation. The purpose of evangelical ethics is to interpret not a set of rules but the gift of freedom, and in particular the call to human action which is implied in this gift.

John Newton Thomas
Thomas Wieser

CONTENTS

EVANGELICAL THEOLOGY
IN THE 19TH CENTURY

EVANGELICAL THEOLOGY
IN THE 19TH CENTURY*

"Theology," in the literal sense, means the science and doctrine of God. A very precise definition of the Christian endeavor in this respect would really require the more complex term "The-anthropology." For an abstract doctrine of God has no place in the Christian realm, only a "doctrine of God and of man," a doctrine of the commerce and communion between God and man.

"Evangelical" means informed by the gospel of Jesus Christ, as heard afresh in the 16th-century Reformation by direct return to Holy Scripture.

"Evangelical theology" must thus be understood as the science and doctrine of the commerce and communion between God and man, informed by the gospel of Jesus Christ as heard in Holy Scripture.

Evangelical theology according to this definition did exist in the 19th century. As part of the "panorama" of this era, along with much natural science and technology, history and politics, literature, art and philosophy, and along with Roman Catholic theology, this evangelical theology was present. My task here is to describe it briefly. I shall confine myself to the German-speaking world. This is justified in that 19th-century German theology was the signpost for theological endeavor elsewhere. This pre-eminence may not last indefinitely.

The 19th century is behind us. So also is the evangelical

* Address given by Karl Barth at the meeting of the *Goethegesellschaft* in Hannover, January 8, 1957, and entitled "Panorama of a Century."

theology of that century. The breach separating us from the
19th century is perhaps more pronounced in the field of
theology than in any other academic discipline, although it
is nowhere absent. This is not to say that 19th-century theology is to be dismissed. Such a procedure would be out of
order in any academic discipline, but most certainly in theology. Theology belongs to the wider realm of the Christian
Church, ecumenical and universal, in space as well as in time.
In the Church there exists a community of concern that may
be endangered, but never cancelled out, by even the most
serious differences in approach. In the Church and hence in
theology the commandment, "Honor thy father and thy
mother," is valid, and this commandment remains binding on
the children even when they have left their parents' house. To
respect and sustain the ties that bind the present to the past, in
spite of deep breaches, is therefore imperative. Evangelical
theology of today has additional and for us more urgent tasks
than those of the 19th century. But the 19th century's tasks
remain for us, too. However different our approach, we cannot and must not abandon these tasks of a bygone day. To do
so does not, I suppose, serve the purpose of any discipline; it
certainly does not serve theology well.

Let us begin with some summary remarks about the history
of evangelical theology in the 19th century.

There is hardly any doubt that the distinctive beginnings
of 19th-century theology coincide with the publication of
Schleiermacher's book *On Religion, Speeches to Its Cultured
Despisers* in 1799. Whoever wishes to know and to understand this theology must read this little book with great care,
though it is by no means easily digested. It clearly shows the
breach separating the new theology at that time from both
17th-century Orthodoxy and 18th-century Enlightenment and
Pietism.

[handwritten margin note: History of theology is the parent of contemporary theology]

The *course* of the history of 19th-century theology is fairly obvious from there on, at least in its main outline. In its understanding of Christian man, this theology was first animated and nourished by Herder and the Romantics, as well as by the religious and national awakening of the Napoleonic era. Subsequently, it found its splendid foundation and means of expression through speculative Idealism, through Hegel's version of it in particular, even though it came to be subjected to severe criticism from this very source. Under the increasing pressure of advancing positivism in the second half of the century—here the name of Albrecht Ritschl is to be remembered—theology retreated to the epistomology and ethics of Kant rediscovered, and to an interpretation of Luther rediscovered in the light of Kant. Finally, only a small realm remained for the genuine religious experience of the individual. Theology turned into philosophy of the history of religion in general, and of the Christian religion in particular.

The 19th century also had its outsiders. I mention Johann Christoph Blumhardt, Hermann Friedrich Kohlbrügge, Wilhelm Löhe and, for the final years, the quite different Franz Overbeck. Perhaps Johann Tobias Beck and Adolf Schlatter should be included here. These outsiders fitted only partially or not at all into the main development. Since they were either overlooked or viewed with condescension by their contemporaries, they in no way halted or even interrupted the main course. Kierkegaard in particular did not have the slightest influence on 19th-century theology, except, again, in the case of a few individuals. True, there was a more conservative element which was tied more strictly to the Bible and the traditional teachings of the Church; there was also a more progressive element, more liberal in its relationship to those authorities; furthermore, there were between them a number of theologies of mediation. But these elements were variations within the same general trend. None of them broke up the rather uniform picture even though there were occasional violent clashes. Incidentally, the theological leadership came undoubtedly from among the liberals. It was the liberals who raised the questions and answered them in a way which was characteristic for the century as a whole.

It may be much more difficult to come to an agreement as to the *eclipse* of this theology. The year 1900 brought the 19th century to its chronological end and marked at the same time a climax in the history of its theology: the publication of Harnack's *What Is Christianity?* Due to this achievement, 19th-century theology continued to live for some time with force and dignity almost unbroken, in spite of signs of dissolution. This made possible a shortlived and partial renaissance of Schleiermacher around 1910. The actual end of the 19th century as the "good old days" came for theology as for everything else with the fateful year of 1914. Accidentally or not, a significant event took place during that very year. Ernst Troeltsch, the well-known professor of systematic theology and the leader of the then most modern school, gave up his chair in theology for one in philosophy. One day in early August 1914 stands out in my personal memory as a black day. Ninety-three German intellectuals impressed public opinion by their proclamation in support of the war policy of Wilhelm II and his counselors. Among these intellectuals I discovered to my horror almost all of my theological teachers whom I had greatly venerated. In despair over what this indicated about the signs of the time I suddenly realized that I could not any longer follow either their ethics and dogmatics or their understanding of the Bible and of history. For me at least, 19th-century theology no longer held any future. For many, if not for most people, this theology did not become again what it had been, once the waters of the flood descending

upon us at that time had somewhat receded. Everything has
its time. Evangelical theology in the true spirit and style of the
19th century continued to exist and some vestiges still remain.
But in its former wholeness it is a cause which today is significantly represented by only a few. This is not to say that
we do not owe it our most serious attention for our own sake
and for the sake of the future. But it remains true that the
history of this theology had its beginnings, its various peaks,
and then also its end. ⌐→distinguishes 19ᶜ theology

One respectful statement must be added immediately at
this point. Time made it unusually difficult for this theology to
be developed and get a hearing, let alone to get accepted, beyond its own proper realm in the various Protestant churches.
Nineteenth-century theology was burdened with the heritage
of the 18th century. There was an all-pervasive rationalism
and a retreat of vital or would-be vital Christianity into un-
dergrounds of many kinds. These factors, coupled with the
emergence of obscure forms of religious fanaticism, led to a
kind of secularism probably more pointed than the much
praised or deplored secularism of today. In addition, theology
was measured against the impressive achievements and per-
sonalities of the so-called classical era of German culture,
philosophic and poetic; against the breathtaking political
movements of the war of liberation 1813-15, followed by
the years of revolution and restoration, the foundation-laying
of the empires, and the subsequent repercussions of all these
events down to World War I. Above all, theology was measured against the all-embracing triumphs of the natural sci-
ences, of philosophy of history, of modern technology, as
well as against Beethoven, Wagner, and Brahms, Gottfried
Keller and Theodor Fontane, Ibsen and Sudermann. What
did theology have to say to this century—not to speak of the
shadow of Goethe and Bismarck and Friedrich Nietzsche—

with its many-sided interest busily and progressively occupied elsewhere, to readers of the *Gartenlaube*, of the *Daheim*, and later of the *Kunstwart** who numbered among them the more or less zealous Christians? What did this theology have to offer to a man who gave no thought to eternity, surrounded as he was by the riches of his time; who was firmly grounded in unshakable self-assurance, as was the case with the average man of the 19th century? Such a man would take notice of theology only if and when it suited his own radical or reactionary purposes, but he had so many objections to it that his indifference occasionally turned into open aversion and hostility. Whatever one may think of the presuppositions, methods, and results of these 19th-century evangelical theologians, it was an act of intellectual and, in the last analysis, of spiritual steadfastness that they were not afraid to face this modern man. They did so much more directly than their Roman Catholic counterparts because they dared to expose themselves to this climate as they carried through their work. This achievement must be seen and acknowledged before we disagree with these theologians and depart from their positions.

One must speak with equal reverence of the human and scientific attitude of many if not all of the representatives of this theology. From Schleiermacher and his melancholy friend De Wette in Basel down to Richard Rothe, Isaak August Dorner, Ferdinand Christian Baur, Hoffman and Frank of Erlangen, Alexander Schweizer and Alois Emanuel Biedermann in Zurich, to Martin Kaehler, Ludwig Ihmels, Adolf von Harnack, Wilhelm Herrmann, and finally to the last great liberal, Hermann Lüdemann, who was driven from Holstein and went to Berne—what scholarly figures they were, each in

---

* *Kunstwart, Gartenlaube,* and *Daheim* were German weeklies or monthlies for art and literature.

his own way, educated and cultivated, well grounded and well rounded! Those of us who knew some of them will know what I mean when I say that from many of these persons there emanated an unforgettable air of conscientiousness, of churchly and spontaneous piety, of a peculiar combination of ethical earnestness and academic dignity. All this exists today only in weak imitations and as such might better not exist at all. I say this in order to emphasize that in dealing with the theologians of the 19th century, at least with the best among them, we are faced with a type of person that merits our highest respect. This in itself is reason enough for our listening to them even today. Another question is then certainly in order: whether these theologians may not have been a little too serious at being professors, taking themselves too seriously. Serenity is not the strongest impression we gain from their writings, and while several had a sense of humor it easily became a trifle bilious when it was allowed to assert itself outside their private life. In contrast to their strong scientific self-assurance, a silent anxiety and oppression seems to pervade the physical and mental picture of more than one of them. This should not be a reproach. We have lived through harder times, have endured worse things than they did, and we are thereby, strangely enough, made more free. We are removed from certain battles and involvements in which they were caught in the course of their opposition to and conversation with their apparently sunny age. We can breathe more freely, just because the air has become more raw. Modern man can no longer impress us, as he impressed them, in the light of his performances in this century. In the midst of so much happily rambling and triumphant idealism, materialism, naturalism, skepticism, and other so-called realisms, one can easily become melancholy, and the evangelical theologians probably did as well as they could at that time, both as persons and as scholars.

I shall now turn to a necessarily sketchy survey of the most important and significant problems 19th-century theology had to face. What problems were foremost in the minds of the theologians during all phases of 19th-century development, and how did they master them?

The key problem arose from the conviction that the guiding principle of theology must be confrontation with the contemporary age and its various conceptions, self-understandings, and self-evidences, its genuine and less genuine "movements," its supposed or real progress. True, theology was also at work in and for the Church; it was also concerned with its own proper center, the gospel of Jesus Christ and the faith responding to it; it was concerned with searching and explaining the Scriptures as the document of this gospel, with the history of the Church, founded and determined by this gospel, with her doctrine and her life, with intellectual and systematic formulation of Biblical truth, and with seeking and finding new ways of proclaiming it. However, the theologians had their eyes fixed on the world, and their thinking was necessarily conditioned by this outlook. They wrestled with the challenging issues of their times. Theology—and this was its strength—exposed itself to the world, as its most outstanding spokesmen and achievements demonstrate. Obviously theology has always been to some extent open toward and related to the world, consciously or unconsciously. It should be so. Retreats behind Chinese Walls never served theology well. It must be engaged in conversation with the contemporary world, whatever the means of the dialogue. Whoever denies this may read Schleiermacher, De Wette, Richard Rothe, and study the volumes of the *Christliche Welt*, edited by Martin Rade! The lazy man may learn thereby what openmindedness is! In this respect evangelical theology of the 19th century set an example never to be ignored in any vital theology.

Theology, however, went overboard—and this was its weakness—insofar as confrontation with the contemporary age was its *decisive* and *primary* concern. This was true not only, as happened so often, when it addressed the outside world *ex professo*, in the form of so-called apologetics, but also when it dealt with the questions most proper to itself. Theology never failed to react, whether approvingly or disapprovingly, critically or uncritically, to impulses from outside, at times even with extreme nervousness. This openness to the world meant (1) that through the open windows and doors came so much stimulation for thought and discussion that there was hardly time or love or zeal left for the task to be accomplished within the house itself. With all its energies captivated by the world, 19th-century theology achieved surprisingly little in terms of a new and positive understanding of Christian truth and truths in themselves, a primary necessity at all times. The winds were enthusiastically welcomed and allowed to enter freely through the outside doors. This meant (2) that not a few doors inside were slammed which should have been kept open as well. Nineteenth-century theology ascribed normative character to the ideas of its environment. Consequently it was forced to make reductions and oversimplifications, to indulge in forgetfulness and carelessness, when it dealt with the exciting and all-important matters of Christian understanding. These developments were bound to threaten, indeed to undermine, both theology and the Church with impoverishment and triviality. The outside winds brought not merely fresh air, but also notoriously foul air. This meant (3) that fatal errors blew in, were admitted, and made themselves at home. These errors, far from being simply tolerated, enjoyed birthright, even authority. Countereffects to be sure were not lacking, but there was no fundamental agreement about the absolute primacy of the positive tasks of theology in and for the

Church, over against the secondary tasks of relating to the various philosophies of the times. Finally, we miss a certain carefree and joyful confidence in the self-validation of the basic concerns of theology, a trust that the most honest commerce with the world might best be assured when the theologians, unheeding the favors or disfavors of this world, confronted it with the results of theological research carried out for its own sake. It did not enter their minds that respectable dogmatics could be good apologetics. Man in the 19th century might have taken the theologians more seriously if they themselves had not taken him so seriously. Even the best representatives of this theology have never overcome this limitation, in spite of their exemplary openness to the world. And this was the key problem of 19th-century theology.

This general assumption of openness to the world led necessarily to the specific assumption that theology could defend its own cause only within the framework of a total view of man, the universe, and God which could command universal recognition. How could the theologians establish and preserve the much-coveted contact with the contemporary world if they did not speak from within one of the current philosophies and world views, granted certain reservations and modifications? The validity of the Christian message was at stake, or more precisely the possibility of a voluntary but universal acceptance of its validity. Theoretically, Protestantism has always maintained that no outward or inward pressure can or should be brought upon anyone to accept the Christian message and with it the Christian faith. While this had often been overlooked in practice by Protestantism in earlier centuries, it had rightly become commonplace for the theologians of the 19th as well as the 18th century. Quite rightly these theologians stressed the possibility of free response offered to all men, including their contemporaries. We can only do justice to the fundamental significance of their efforts if we understand them against the background of the missionary and evangelistic concern which is characteristic of modern Christianity: the Christian obligation rediscovered in the 18th century to call and invite all men, near and far, to the free acceptance of the validity of the message of Jesus Christ and thus to faith in Him. So far, so good.

The theologians of the 19th century proceeded fundamentally along the lines of the 18th-century Christian Enlightenment. Their particular venture became questionable, however, as they set out to prove the possibility of faith in its relatedness to, and its conditioning by, the world views which were normative for their contemporaries and even for themselves. More precisely, they tried to find that point of reference in the world views where voluntary acceptance of the Christian message and the Christian faith suggested themselves more or less convincingly and were viewed at least as possibilities. It is evident that for this purpose the theologians had to make a particular world view their own and had to affirm its validity. This was all the easier for them as acceptance of a prevailing philosophy was precisely the presupposition for their work. The world views changed in the course of the century; but there were always theologians who went along, more or less convinced, if not enthusiastic, and who started the theological task afresh within the new framework.

In contrast to Enlightenment theology, the 19th-century theologians focused their attention on one particular point in relation to all the various world views of their time: man's supposedly innate and essential capacity to "sense and taste the infinite" as Schleiermacher said, or the "religious a priori" as later affirmed by Troeltsch. There was scarcely a theologian who did not also consider himself a professional philosopher. These philosophers of religion, more or less faithful or so-

phisticated advocates of one of the current world views, were
busily working out a general epistomology, a system of meta-
physics and ethics focusing on this very capacity. In these
terms they sought to validate the potential for religion, including the Christian faith. The great efforts undertaken in the
steps of Schleiermacher by men like De Wette, Biedermann,
Lipsius, Kaftan, and Lüdemann were highly commendable.

And yet these efforts were surrounded by two questions
which we may find difficult to answer in the affirmative.

First! Were men prepared to take such lessons from the
theologians? Did they permit having their world views sup-
plemented? Were they sensitive to man's openness toward
religion and the Christian faith, and desirous to make any use
of it? The revelation theology of Schelling during his later
years should not be forgotten at this point. And we must not
overlook that later philosophers like Lotze, Siebeck, Dilthey,
and Eucken actively shared in their own way in the work of
the theologians. But it was a bad omen that Goethe, in whose
name we are gathered here, either ignored or viewed with
displeasure what was happening. He disliked Schleiermacher's
Speeches, quite apart from their romantic garb. The same can
be said of Hegel, the other great master of the century.
The efforts of Schleiermacher and of his successors did not
acquire any significance for the broad mass of the "cultured"
to whom Schleiermacher had addressed himself so impressively
with his proof of the roots of religion in the structure of
man's spiritual life. The thinking of the awakening labor class
of the 19th century was even less influenced. The gratitude
showered upon the theologians by the groups they addressed
was not really encouraging. If this does not necessarily speak
against the excellency of what these philosopher-theologians
did, it is yet a quite serious matter when compared with the
explicit intention of their work.

The second question is more serious. Could the Christian message and the Christian faith be a subject for debate while the validity of a general world view was presupposed? Is there any proof that acceptance of a particular world view will make Christianity generally accessible or even possible? Even granted the existence of man's religious disposition, can the Christian faith be called one of its expressions, in other words a "religion"? Nineteenth-century evangelical theology assumed that this was so. But it could not do so without subjugating the Christian message and the Christian faith to that interpretation and form by which Christianity could achieve validity and general accessibility for the proponents of the prevailing world view. The Christian faith had to be understood as a "religion" if it was to be generally accepted as valid. What if it resisted this classification? What if acceptance was so eagerly sought that Christian faith ceased to be Christian faith as soon as it was interpreted as "religion"? What if the attempt to give it the "firm" basis actually removed the real ground from under it? Nineteenth-century theology did not raise these questions. One wonders, therefore, whether its most typical spokesmen were not primarily philosophers and only secondarily theologians. This might explain the failure of their missionary task at a deeper level. Was it possible to win the "gentiles" for the Christian cause by first accepting the "gentile" point of view, in order to commend to them the Christian cause? Could this procedure impress the "gentiles"? Would it not have been necessary first to be innocent as doves in order to be wise as serpents?

Nineteenth-century theology worked on the general assumption that relatedness to the world is its primary task and on the specific assumption that there is a possibility for general acceptance of the Christian faith. The result was that the theologians, when they came to work on their proper task in and for the Church, were more interested in the Christian faith than in the Christian message. In terms of content they were more interested in man's relationship to God than in God's dealings with man, or, to quote the well-known term of Melanchthon, more in the *beneficia Christi* than in Christ Himself. This emphasis informed their interpretation of the Bible, their positive or critical attitude toward the early dogmas, and the confessions of the Reformation. It informed their research in, and their exposition of, church history and finally their own formulation of the Christian faith. The interest of these theologians focused on the believing man in his past and in his present, in his confrontation and association with Jesus Christ. Theological discussion with the contemporary world centered around the existence of the believing man, and in philosophy of religion particularly around the possibility of this existence. The prevailing interest in this direction would not necessarily have been erroneous had it been a matter of shift in tone and emphasis for serious and pertinent reasons. The Bible speaks emphatically of the commerce of the believing Israelite and the believing Christian with God and therefore of the believing man as such. How else could it testify on behalf of Him who was very God and very man? The theologians should not have hesitated so long to appeal to Luther, especially the early Luther, and to the early Melanchthon! And how much assistance and guidance could they have received had they paid any attention to Kierkegaard! There is no reason why the attempt of Christian anthropocentrism should not be made, indeed ought not to be made. There is certainly a place for legitimate Christian thinking starting from below and moving up, from man who is taken hold of by God to God who takes hold of man. Let us interpret this attempt by the 19th-century theologians in its best light! Provided that it in no way claims to be exclusive and absolute, one might well understand it as an attempt to formulate a theology of the third article of the Apostles' Creed, the Holy Spirit. If it had succeeded in this, 19th-century theology could have irrevocably stressed once again the fact that we cannot consider God's commerce with man without concurrently considering man's commerce with God. Theology is in reality not only the doctrine of God, but the doctrine of God and man. Interpreted in this light, 19th-century theology would not have forgotten or even suppressed, but rather stressed, the fact that man's relation to God is based on God's dealings with man, and not conversely. Starting from below, as it were, with Christian man, it could and should have struggled its way upward to an authentic explication of the Christian faith. It could and should have sought increasingly to validate the Christian message as God's act and word, the ground, object, and content of faith.

Hoffmann of Erlangen, a Lutheran, must have had such an upswing in his mind when he made the daring attempt to portray the movement from man to God in the whole Bible and to get at the Scriptures as testimony of the divinely initiated and governed history leading to the ultimate salvation of man (*Heilsgeschichte*). He did this in terms of his self-consciousness as a Christian. But insofar as Hoffmann's theology was intended to be a theology of Christian self-understanding and not a theology of the Holy Spirit, it could not break through the general trend of the century. This is true in spite of the significance which this theology has for us even today. The basic concern of evangelical theology could not find a genuine expression in these terms. If only the need for an approach from below had been genuine and had grown out of a new examination of the authentic concerns of theology! However, it unabashedly originated from borrowed presuppositions. This movement of thought from man to God became exclusive and absolute. Nineteenth-century theologians spoke of "faith," and we do well to trust that they meant Christian faith. But their assumptions compelled them to understand faith as the realization of one form of man's spiritual life and self-awareness. The more serious they were in this interpretation, the more the Christian faith appeared to be a windowless monad, dependent on human feelings, knowledge, and will. Like these, faith was supposed to be self-nurturing, self-governing, and self-sufficient. A capacity for the infinite within the finite, faith had no ground, object, or content other than itself. It had no vis-à-vis. Faith as the Christian's commerce with God could first and last be only the Christian's commerce with himself. It could express only itself, its own inner dialectics, in so many words and sentences. How could the truth of the Christian gospel be asserted except by understanding it and interpreting it as a statement, an expression, a predicate, or a symbol of the Christian's inner experience? Theology was still being penalized for accepting the Renaissance discovery that man was the measure of all things, including Christian things. On this ground the testimony of Christian faith, however honest, and however richly endowed with Biblical and Reformation recollections, could only exist like a fish out of water. On this ground there was no effective answer to be given to Feuerbach who eagerly invoked Luther's sanction in support of his theory that statements of the Christian faith, like those of all other religions, are in reality statements of more or less profound human needs and desires projected into the infinite. Christian dogmatics was especially hard put during this period to raise any interesting and provocative questions, and to provide vital answers. By the time it had dealt with the philosophical presuppositions and the historical-critical problems, its voice was subdued and bare of enthusiasm. Was it at all worth the trouble publicly to discuss a man's inner experiences even if he was a Christian? Was such a self-revelation on the basis of self-knowledge at all possible? May not man be more hidden from man, the Christian from other Christians, than God is hidden from man? These questions, too, were among those which 19th-century theology never raised because it saw no problem in this direction.

However, theology could hardly improve its position among the other academic disciplines, much as it so desired, as long as it could give as the reason for its particular existence merely a specific human self-understanding and expression. Another consequence of this religious anthropocentrism was even worse. It has already been said that when the Christian gospel was changed into a statement, a religion, about Christian self-awareness, the God was lost sight of who in His sovereignty confronts man, calling him to account, and dealing with him as Lord. This loss also blurred the sight horizontally. The Christian was condemned to uncritical and irresponsible subservience to the patterns, forces, and movements of human history and civilization. Man's inner experience did not provide a firm enough ground for resistance to these phenomena. Deprived of a guiding principle man could turn anywhere. It was fatal for the evangelical Church and for Christianity in the 19th century that theology in the last analysis had nothing more to offer than the "human," the "religious," mystery and its noncommittal "statements," leaving the faithful to whatever impressions and influences from outside proved strongest.

How confused was the position of the evangelical Church in regard to changing world views! How long did it take the Church to become concerned about social questions, to take socialism seriously, and with how much spiritual dilettantism was this finally done! How naively did the Church subscribe to political conservatism in the first half of the century and in the second half to the preservation of the liberal bourgeoisie, the growing nationalism and militarism! All this certainly not with ill will; but theologically the ship was without a rudder. And he who in 1933 may still have been spellbound by the theology of the 19th century was hopelessly condemned, save for a special intervention of grace, to bet on the wrong horse in regard to national socialism and during the clash between the Confessing Church and the German Christians who supported the new regime (*Kirchenkampf*). I mention these developments only as symptoms. As indications of the situation brought about by the religious anthropocentrism of 19th-century theology they needed mentioning.

I would like to make some final remarks. Mindful of its origins in Herder and the Romanticists, 19th-century theology has given new emphasis and recognition to the essentially historical nature of the Christian faith which sets Christianity apart from other religions. This is the merit and achievement of this theology. Christian faith is shaped by its relationship to the history which finds its central meaning in the name of Jesus Christ. For this very reason Biblical exegesis and the study of the history of the Church and its dogmas were bound to become again urgent and distinctive tasks. The path to be followed in this attempt to do justice to the historicity of Christianity was irrevocably given by the presuppositions upon which 19th-century theology operated. Its spokesmen had no choice but to understand the Christian faith, in its essence, as a series of historical phenomena: Christianity a particular religion alongside other religions and in the context of the general history of religions; past patterns and expressions of Christianity; and finally the history which finds its central meaning in the name of Jesus Christ, His person and His life, the original phenomenon of faith so to speak, but never more than a *historical* phenomenon. The theologians had to apprehend Him—or should we say, to lay hold of Him?—historically, that is in terms of the history of religions and according to the historical-critical method prevailing at that time. They had to approach the person and the life of Jesus on the basis of the New Testament record, but they also had to distinguish His own religion from that of His witnesses and their environment. Furthermore, they had to establish and to evaluate these corollary religious events, both in their particular characteristics and in their relationship to the original event of Jesus Christ. They had to trace the forms of faith in the Church down through the centuries in their variety and in their continuing development. Informed by the results of this research, they had to ascertain the contemporary form of Christian faith. In this historical-critical undertaking, 19th-century theology enjoyed without reservation the confrontation and the formal agreement with the conceptions and ways of thought of the environment. Theology met the test as a science, and brilliantly so in the life work of men—to again mention only a few—like Ferdinand Christian Baur, Karl August von Hase, Heinrich Julius Holtzmann, Adolf Jülicher, Adolf von Harnack, Karl Holl, Ernst Troeltsch; one should also remember to give honor to Theodor Zahn, on the conservative side. In the light of the general and of the specific assumptions of 19th-century theology, the historical determination of the Christian faith became visible in the results of the research of these men. These results were constantly vacillating, contested, and subject to discussion, and some were truly amazing and caused vexation or rejoicing, depending on one's outlook. I remember for instance when I was a student at Berne, Rudolf Steck, one of the very dignified last disciples of the so-called Tübingen School, suggesting, if not teaching, that not only several of the Pauline letters, but every one of them, might be "false," might be products of the second century. And we all know of the famous *Life of Jesus* by David Friedrich Strauss who gave one of the strongest impulses to the theological enterprise by his attempt to prove the mythical character of even the Christ phenomenon! Even in the cautious and moderate research of the majority of the scholars along the main roads there was curtailing, rationalizing, psychologizing, and demythologizing going on!

Important for the total picture, however, were not the sometimes more radical, sometimes more conservative, results of this research, but rather the fundamental questions which were triumphantly bypassed. Was Jesus Christ really nothing more than the original phenomenon of Christian faith? Was He not to be comprehended as its ground, content, and object on the basis of the first records—the New Testament—as well as of the later accounts—those of the Church—varied and conditioned by their time as they were? Was, therefore, Christ's historical existence at all accessible to a research which reached beyond the texts of the New Testament? What if the structure of these texts disqualified them as a proper "source" for use by neutral historical science? This question was persistently raised by Martin Kaehler in the 19th century, but it received no attention. Furthermore, were the theologians not doomed to misread the New Testament texts in their attempt at understanding them as documents of certain religious phenomena? Finally, with this purpose in mind could they possibly expect to understand the documents of Church history and of the history of doctrine? Was this endeavor truly what it claimed to be, a genuinely historical one? Did not the whole enterprise, from beginning to end, painfully suffer from the fundamental mistake that, in the words of Schleiermacher, productive theologizing was possible only from a lofty place "above" Christianity? What if by talking

about Christianity as a religion these theologians had already
ceased to speak of Christianity and hence were unable to
communicate the faith with authority to those on the outside?
What if the only relevant way of speaking of Christianity
was from within? We do not fail to pay due tribute to the
"historical-critical" theology for the valuable stimulation,
illumination, and guidance it offered with regard to the Bible
and Church history. But it did so only insofar as it was not
merely a "historical-critical" method but was *nolens volens*
theology, above all insofar as its *subject matter* was powerful
enough to break through the questionable vehicles of 19th-
century research and speak for itself. Except for this fact,
since otherwise it was nothing more than "historical-critical"
research and doctrine, forsaken by God and the Spirit, 19th-
century theology would not have been able to offer any
Christian truth of importance and of historical relevancy. If it
had been allowed to run its full course, the Christian faith
would no longer have been subjected to the history which
finds its central meaning in the name of Jesus Christ. On the
contrary, this history would have become subjected to the
interpretation by the particular mode of Christian religion
which the theologians equated with the Christian faith.

   A deplorable consequence must be mentioned with reference to this last point. Nineteenth-century theology appeared
to the outside world mainly as history of religion. This may
have been the reason for the mutual indifference which ex-
isted, at least during the second half of the century, between
evangelical theology and Roman Catholic theology. It is de-
batable whether this indifference was an improvement over
the vivid and so much complained-about hostilities of earlier
times which at least indicated mutual interest. Roman Catholic
theology, too, underwent strange developments in the beginning of the century, and these were in part strikingly similar

to those of Protestantism. However, in the era of Pius IX it regained its peculiar balance through a far from exemplary return to Thomism. Obviously evangelical theology, considered as a discipline of the history of religion, had no choice but to interpret the conduct of its opponent as an uncritical and unhistorical dealing with authority and hence reminiscent of the Dark Ages. Conversely, Roman Catholic theology had to condemn the endeavor of evangelical theology as irresponsible surrender and secularization of the historical character of the Christian faith. A dialogue between these two partners which would have gone beyond the shouting back and forth of slogans was as impossible as a conversation between an elephant and a whale. The relationship did not even take the form of meaningful polemics, let alone the willingness to listen to one another, to learn from one another, to seek and to maintain the ecumenical contacts within the limits of the possible. Who among the evangelicals ever read Catholic dogmatics—and which Roman Catholic ever looked into our expositions of the faith, our *"Glaubenslehren"*? No wonder that both partners turned their backs on each other with the gesture and the prayer of thanksgiving of the Pharisee in the Temple. Could and should this go on? If history of religion on our side (and Neo-Thomism on the other) was the last word of wisdom, the indifference was bound to continue.

I am at the end. It has been my task to give a report on the evangelical theology in the 19th century. Therefore, I was not and I am not now under any obligation to tell you, or even to indicate how this history continued. It would be interesting to hear what a wiser man than myself will have to say about its development a hundred years from now. The history did go on. There is even a certain continuity in spite of inevitable discontinuity. I repeat: the 19th century is *not* to be dismissed, nor is its theology. I could not follow the rule *De mortuis nihil nisi bene* (speak nothing but good of the dead) simply because the theologians of that time are not dead. "In Him they all have life," in the greatness and within the limitations in which they once lived. *Et lux perpetua lucet eis* (and the eternal light shines upon them). And thus they live, excitingly enough, also for us. They will not cease to speak to us. And we cannot cease to listen to them.

THE HUMANITY OF GOD

THE HUMANITY OF GOD*

The humanity of God! Rightly understood that is bound
to mean God's relation to and turning toward man. It signifies
the God who speaks with man in promise and command. It
represents God's existence, intercession, and activity for man,
the intercourse God holds with him, and the free grace in
which He wills to be and is nothing other than the God of
man.

Surely I do not deceive myself when I assume that our
theme today should suggest a *change of direction*† in the
thinking of evangelical theology. We are or ought now
to be engaged in this change, not in opposition to but none
the less in *distinction* from an earlier change. What began
forcibly to press itself upon us about forty years ago was not
so much the humanity of God as His *deity*—a God absolutely
unique in His relation to man and the world, overpoweringly
lofty and distant, strange, yes even wholly other. Such was
the God with whom man has to do when he takes the name
of God upon his lips, when God encounters him, when he
enters into relation with God. We were confronted by the
mystery comparable only to the impenetrable darkness of
death, in which God veils Himself precisely when He unveils,
announces, and reveals Himself to man, and by the judgment
man must experience because God is gracious to him, because
He wills to be and is his God. What we discovered in the
change which occurred at that time was the majesty of the

---

* A lecture delivered at the meeting of the Swiss Reformed Ministers'
Association in Aarau, on September 25th, 1956.
† German: *Wendung.*

crucified, so evident in its full horror, just as Grünewald saw and depicted Him. We saw the finger of John the Baptist, by the same artist, pointing with authority to this holy One: "He must increase but I must decrease."

Unmistakably for us the *humanity* of God at that time moved from the center to the periphery, from the emphasized principal clause to the less emphasized subordinate clause. I should indeed have been somewhat embarrassed if one had invited me to speak on the humanity of God—say in the year 1920, the year in which I stood up in this hall against my great teacher, Adolf von Harnack. We should have suspected evil implications in this topic. In any case we were not occupied with it. That it is our subject for today and that I could not refuse to say something on it is a symptom of the fact that that earlier change of direction was not the last word. It could not be. Similarly, the change in which we are now engaged cannot be the last word. That, however, may become the concern of another generation. Our problem is this: to derive the knowledge of the humanity of God from the knowledge of His deity.

I

Permit me to give my exposition of this theme first in the form of a report. In a consideration of the earlier change referred to above, a viewpoint regarding the urgent new task of the succeeding period and of today will emerge.

The change of direction then made had a pronounced *critical* and *polemic* character. It came to completion gradually when viewed in terms of time, but as a sudden conversion when viewed in terms of content. It was a precipitous break with the ruling theology of the time, a theology more or less liberal—or even orthodox—representing the climax of a development which had successfully asserted itself for two or three centuries, apparently incapable of being arrested. We are called upon today to accord to that earlier theology, and the entire development culminating in it, greater historical justice than appeared to us possible and feasible in the violence of the first break-off and clash. This is an easier task today than it would have been earlier. However, even in the most un-biased evaluation of its legitimate purpose and its unmistakable service, even in the most peaceful review of it, one cannot hide the fact that it could no longer continue as it was. Modification of the theological conception then normative through new and at the same time older and original Christian knowledge and ways of speaking proved unavoidable. Evangelical theology almost all along the line, certainly in all its representative forms and tendencies, had become *religionistic*, *anthropocentric*, and in this sense *humanistic*. What I mean to say is that an external and internal disposition and emotion of man, namely his piety—which might well be Christian piety—had become its object of study and its theme. Around this it revolved and seemed compelled to revolve without release. This was true of evangelical theology in its doctrine of principles, in its presentation of the Christian past and its practical understanding of the Christian present, in its ethics and in that which perhaps was to be regarded as its dogmatics, in the proclamation and instruction of the Church determined by it—above all, however, in its interpretation of the Bible. What did it know and say of the *deity* of God? For this theology, to think about God meant to think in a scarcely veiled fashion about man, more exactly about the religious, the Christian religious man. To speak about God meant to speak in an exalted tone but once again and more than ever about this man—his revelations and wonders, his faith and his works. There is no question about it: here man was made great at the cost of God—the divine God who is someone other than man, who sovereignly confronts him, who immovably and unchangeably stands over against him as the Lord, Creator, and Redeemer. This God who is also man's free partner in a history inaugurated by Him and in a dialogue ruled by Him was in danger of being reduced, along with this history and this dialogue, to a pious notion—to a mystical expression and symbol of a current alternating between a man and his own heights or depths. But whatever truth was gained in this way could be only that of a monologue.

At this point some of us were appalled after we, along with everyone else, had drained the different chalices of this theology to the last drop. We then concluded (from approximately the middle of the second decade of our century on) that we could not side with it any longer. Why? Had the pious man and the religion of whose history and presence we had heard so many glorious things at the university and of which we ourselves thereafter had tried to speak, become a matter of question in our own person? Was it the encounter with socialism as interpreted by Kutter and Ragaz which opened our eyes to the fact that God might actually be wholly other than the God confined to the musty shell of the Christian-religious self-consciousness, and that as such He might act and speak? Was it the suddenly darkened outlook for the world, in contrast to the long period of peace in our youth, which awakened us to the fact that man's distress might be too great for a reference to his religious potentiality to prove a comforting and prophetic word? Was it—this has played a decisive role for me personally—precisely the failure of the ethics of the modern theology of the time, with the outbreak of the First World War, which caused us to grow puzzled also about its exegesis, its treatment of history, and its dogmatics? Or was it, in a positive sense, the message of Blumhardt concerning the Kingdom of God which, remarkably enough, was only

then becoming timely? Was it Kierkegaard, Dostoevski, Overbeck, read as a commentary on that message, through which
we found ourselves compelled to look for and set sail to new
shores? Or was it something more fundamental than all that,
namely, the discovery that the theme of the Bible, contrary
to the critical and to the orthodox exegesis which we inherited, certainly could not be man's religion and religious morality and certainly not his own secret divinity? The stone wall
we first ran up against was that the theme of the Bible is the
deity of *God*, more exactly God's *deity*—God's independence
and particular character, not only in relation to the natural but
also to the spiritual cosmos; God's absolutely unique existence,
might, and initiative, above all, in His relation to man. Only
in this manner were we able to understand the voice of the
Old and New Testaments. Only with this perspective did we
feel we could henceforth be theologians, and in particular,
preachers—ministers of the divine Word.

Were we right or wrong? We were certainly right! Let one
read the doctrine of Troeltsch and Stephan! Let one read also
the dogmatics of Lüdemann, in its way so solid, or even that
of Seeberg! If all that wasn't a blind alley! Beyond doubt
what was then in order was not some kind of further shifting
around within the complex of inherited questions, as this was
finally attempted by Wobbermin, Schaeder, and Otto, but
rather a change of direction. The ship was threatening to run
aground; the moment was at hand to turn the rudder an angle
of exactly 180 degrees. And in view of what is to be said later,
let it immediately be stated: "That which is gone does not
return." Therefore there never could be a question of denying
or reversing that change. It was, however, later on and it is
today a question of "revision." * A *genuine* revision in no way

---

* German: *Retraktation*, from the Latin, *retractatio*. Barth is thinking of
Augustine's *Retractationes*.

We must say what was said before, but even better.

Fine turn of theology.

Before we only knew of it.

Some of we keep proclaiming to disclose its whole.

involves a subsequent retreat, but rather a new beginning and attack in which what previously has been said is to be said more than ever, but now even <u>better</u>. If that which we then thought we had discovered and brought forth was no last word but one requiring a revision, it was none the less a true word. As such it must remain, and still cannot be bypassed; rather it constitutes the presupposition of that which must be further considered today. He who may not have joined in that earlier change of direction, who still may not be impressed with the fact that God is God, would certainly not see what is now to be said in addition as the true word concerning His humanity.

In regard to the change which then took place one might well have sung:

"See the moon in yonder sky?
'Tis only half that meets the eye." *

It must now quite frankly be granted that we were at that time only partially in the right, even in reference to the theology which we inherited and from which we had to disengage ourselves—partially right in the same sense in which all preponderantly critical-polemic movements, attitudes, and positions, however meaningful they may be, are usually only partially in the right. What expressions we used—in part taken over and in part newly invented!—above all, the famous "wholly other" breaking in upon us "perpendicularly from above," the not less famous "infinite qualitative distinction" between God and man, the vacuum, the mathematical point, and the tangent in which alone they must meet. "And as she warbled, a thousand voices in the field sang it back." † There

---

* From the hymn, "The Moon Has Risen," by Matthius Claudius.
† Emmanuel Geibel.

Theology's problem

was also the bold assurance that there is in the Bible only *one* theological interest, namely, that in God; that only *one* way appears, namely, that from above downwards; that only *one* message can be heard, namely, that of an immediate forgiveness of sins both in prospect and in retrospect. The problem of ethics was identified with man's sickness unto death; redemption was viewed as consisting in the abolition of the creatureliness of the creature, the swallowing of immanence by transcendence, and in conformity with these the demand for a faith like a spring into the abyss, and more of the like! All this, however well it may have been meant and however much it may have mattered, was nevertheless said somewhat severely and brutally, and moreover—at least according to the other side—in part heretically. How we cleared things away! And we did almost nothing but clear away! Everything which even remotely smacked of mysticism and morality, of pietism and romanticism, or even of idealism, was suspected and sharply interdicted or bracketed with reservations which sounded actually prohibitive! What should really have been only a sad and friendly smile was a derisive laugh!

Did not the whole thing frequently seem more like the report of an enormous execution than the message of the Resurrection, which was its real aim? Was the impression of many contemporaries wholly unfounded, who felt that the final result might be to stand Schleiermacher on his head, that is, to make *God* great for a change at the cost of *man?* Were they wrong in thinking that actually not too much had been won and that perhaps in the final analysis it was only a new Titanism at work? Was it only obduracy when, beside the many who to some extent listened with relief and accompanied us, so many others preferred to shake their heads, nonplused or—like Harnack at that time—even angry over such an innovation? Was there not perhaps in their obduracy the dark presentiment that, in the religionism, the anthropocentrism, the ill-fated humanism of the earlier theology, there might have been something at work that could not be given up? Is it possible that, granted the unmistakable contestability, even perversity of their position, the *humanity* of God did not quite come into its rights in the manner in which we, absorbed as we were in contemplation of the mighty deployment of Leviathan and Behemoth in the book of Job, lifted up His deity on the candlestick?

Where did we really go astray? Where was and is the starting point for the new change of direction? The shrewd friend from another shore* has, as is well known, laid his finger on the fact that at that time we worked almost exclusively with the concept of diastasis, only seldom and incidentally with the complementary concept of analogy. That may be the case. But was not this formal principle merely a symptom of a more deep-seated, essential infirmity in our thinking and speaking at that time? I believe it consisted in the fact that we were wrong exactly where we were right, that at first we did not know how to carry through with sufficient care and thoroughness the new knowledge of the *deity* of God which was so exciting both to us and to others. It was certainly good and proper to return to it and to make it known with greater power. Moreover, Master Calvin in particular, has given us more than wise guidance in this matter. The allegation that we were teaching that God is everything and man nothing, was bad. As a matter of fact, certain hymns of praise to humanism were at that time occasionally raised—the Platonic in particular, in which Calvin was nurtured.

It is nevertheless true that it was pre-eminently the image

---

* Hans Urs von Balthasar, a Swiss Roman Catholic priest and author of *Karl Barth: A Presentation and Interpretation of His Theology.*

THE HUMANITY OF GOD   45

and concept of a "wholly other" that fascinated us and which
we, though not without examination, had dared to identify with
the deity of Him who in the Bible is called Yahweh-Kyrios.
We viewed this "wholly other" in isolation, abstracted and
absolutized, and set it over against man, this miserable wretch
—not to say boxed his ears with it—in such fashion that it
continually showed greater similarity to the deity of the God
of the philosophers than to the deity of the God of Abraham,
Isaac, and Jacob. Was there not a threat that a stereotyped
image would arise again? What if the result of the new hymn
to the majesty of God should be a new confirmation of the
hopelessness of all human activity? What if it should issue in
a new justification of the autonomy of man and thus of secularism in the sense of the Lutheran doctrine of the two
kingdoms? That was the concern and the objection of Leon-
hard Ragaz. God forbid! We did not believe nor intend any
such thing.

But did it not appear to escape us by quite a distance that
the *deity* of the *living* God—and we certainly wanted to deal
with Him—found its meaning and its power only in the
context of His history and of His dialogue with *man*, and thus
in His *togetherness* with man? Indeed—and this is the point
back of which we cannot go—it is a matter of *God's* sovereign
togetherness with man, a togetherness grounded in Him and
determined, delimited, and ordered through Him alone. Only
in this way and in this context can it take place and be recognized. It is a matter, however, of God's *togetherness* with
man. Who God is and what He is in His deity He proves and
reveals not in a vacuum as a divine being-for-Himself, but
precisely and authentically in the fact that He exists, speaks,
and acts as the *partner* of man, though of course as the absolutely superior partner. He who does *that* is the living God.
And the freedom in which He does *that* is His deity. It is the

deity which as such also has the character of humanity. In this and only in this form was—and still is—our view of the deity of God to be set in opposition to that earlier theology. There must be positive acceptance and not unconsidered rejection of the elements of truth, which one cannot possibly deny to it even if one sees all its weaknesses. It is precisely God's *deity* which, rightly understood, includes his *humanity*.

II

How do we come to know that? What permits and requires this statement? It is a *Christological* statement, or rather one grounded in and to be unfolded from Christology. A second change of direction after that first one would have been superfluous had we from the beginning possessed the presence of mind to venture the whole inevitable counterthrow from the Christological perspective and thus from the superior and more exact standpoint of the central and entire witness of Holy Scripture. Certainly in *Jesus Christ*, as He is attested in Holy Scripture, we are not dealing with man in the abstract: not with the man who is able with his modicum of religion and religious morality to be sufficient unto himself without God and thus himself to be God. But neither are we dealing with *God* in the abstract: not with one who in His deity exists only separated from man, distant and strange and thus a non-human if not indeed an inhuman God. In Jesus Christ there is no isolation of man from God or of God from man. Rather, in Him we encounter the history, the dialogue, in which God and man meet together and are together, the reality of the covenant *mutually* contracted, preserved, and fulfilled by them. Jesus Christ is in His one Person, as true *God, man's* loyal partner, and as true *man, God's*. He is the Lord humbled for communion with man and likewise the Servant exalted to communion with God. He is the Word spoken from the loftiest, most luminous transcendence and likewise the Word heard in the deepest, darkest immanence. He is both, without their being confused but also without their being divided; He is wholly the one and wholly the other. Thus in this oneness Jesus Christ is the Mediator, the Reconciler, between God and man. Thus He comes forward to *man* on behalf of *God* calling for and awakening faith, love, and hope, and to *God* on behalf of *man*, representing man, making satisfaction and interceding. Thus He attests and guarantees to man God's free *grace* and at the same time attests and guarantees to God man's free *gratitude*. Thus He establishes in His Person the justice of God vis-à-vis man and also the justice of man before God. Thus He is in His Person the covenant in its fullness, the Kingdom of heaven which is at hand, in which God speaks and man hears, God gives and man receives, God commands and man obeys, God's glory shines in the heights and thence into the depths, and peace on earth comes to pass among men in whom He is well pleased. Moreover, exactly in this way Jesus Christ, as this Mediator and Reconciler between God and man, is also the *Revealer* of them both. We do not need to engage in a free-ranging investigation to seek out and construct who and what God truly is, and who and what man truly is, but only to read the truth about both where it resides, namely, in the fullness of their togetherness, their covenant which proclaims itself in Jesus Christ.

Who and what God is—this is what in particular we have to learn better and with more precision in the new change of direction in the thinking and speaking of evangelical theology, which has become necessary in the light of the earlier change. But the question must be, who and what is God *in Jesus Christ*, if we here today would push forward to a better answer.

Beyond doubt God's *deity* is the first and fundamental fact that strikes us when we look at the existence of Jesus Christ as attested in the Holy Scripture. And God's deity in Jesus Christ consists in the fact that God Himself in Him is the *subject* who speaks and acts with sovereignty. *He* is the free One in whom all freedom has its ground, its meaning, its prototype. *He* is the initiator, founder, preserver, and fulfiller of the covenant. *He* is the sovereign Lord of the amazing relationship in which He becomes and is not only different from man but also one with him. *He* is also the creator of him who is His partner. *He* it is through whose faithfulness the corresponding faithfulness of His partner is awakened and takes place. The old Reformed Christology worked that out especially clearly in its doctrine of the "hypostatic union": God is on the throne. In the existence of Jesus Christ, the fact that God speaks, gives, orders, comes absolutely first—that man hears, receives, obeys, can and must only follow this first act. In Jesus Christ man's freedom is wholly enclosed in the freedom of God. Without the condescension of God there would be no exaltation of man. As the Son of God and not otherwise, Jesus Christ is the Son of Man. This sequence is irreversible. God's independence, omnipotence, and eternity, God's holiness and justice and thus God's deity, in its original and proper form, is the power leading to this effective and visible sequence in the existence of Jesus Christ: superiority preceding subordination. Thus we have here no universal deity capable of being reached conceptually, but this concrete deity—real and recognizable in the *descent* grounded in that sequence and peculiar to the existence of Jesus Christ.

But here there is something even more concrete to be seen. God's high freedom in Jesus Christ is His freedom for *love*. The divine capacity which operates and exhibits itself in that superiority and subordination is manifestly also God's capacity

Ascent/descent

to bend downwards, to attach Himself to another and this other to Himself, to be together with him. This takes place in that irreversible sequence, but in it is completely real. In that sequence there arises and continues in Jesus Christ the highest communion of God with man. God's deity is thus no prison in which He can exist only in and for Himself. It is rather His freedom to be in and for Himself but also with and for us, to assert but also to sacrifice Himself, to be wholly exalted but also completely humble, not only almighty but also almighty mercy, not only Lord but also servant, not only judge but also Himself the judged, not only man's eternal king but also his brother in time. And all that without in the slightest forfeiting His deity! All that, rather, in the highest proof and proclamation of His deity! He who *does* and manifestly *can* do all that, He and no other is the living God. So constituted is His deity, the deity of the God of Abraham, Isaac, and Jacob. In Jesus Christ it is in this way operative and recognizable. If He is the Word of Truth, then the truth of *God* is exactly this and nothing else.

It is when we look at Jesus Christ that we know decisively that God's deity does not exclude, but includes His *humanity*. Would that Calvin had energetically pushed ahead on this point in his Christology, his doctrine of God, his teaching about predestination, and then logically also in his ethics! His Geneva would then not have become such a gloomy affair. His letters would then not have contained so much bitterness. It would then not be so easy to play a Heinrich Pestalozzi and, among his contemporaries, a Sebastian Castellio off against him. How could God's deity exclude His humanity, since it is God's freedom for love and thus His capacity to be not only in the heights but also in the depths, not only great but also small, not only in and for Himself but also with another distinct from Him, and to offer Himself to him? In His deity there is enough room for communion with man. Moreover God has and retains in His relation to this other one the unconditioned priority. It is His act. *His* is and remains the first and decisive Word, *His* the initiative, *His* the leadership. How could we see and say it otherwise when we look at Jesus Christ in whom we find man taken up into communion with God? No, God requires no exclusion of humanity, no non-humanity, not to speak of inhumanity, in order to be truly God. But we may and must, however, look further and recognize the fact that actually His deity *encloses humanity in itself*. This is not the fatal Lutheran doctrine of the two natures and their properties. On the contrary, the essential aim of this doctrine is not to be denied at this point but to be adopted. It would be the false deity of a false God if in His deity His humanity did not also immediately encounter us. Such false deities are by Jesus Christ once for all made a laughingstock. In Him the fact is once for all established that God does not exist without man.

It is not as though God stands in need of another as His partner, and in particular of man, in order to be truly God. "What is man, that thou art mindful of him, and the son of man that thou dost care for him?" Why should God not also be able, as eternal Love, to be sufficient unto Himself? In His life as Father, Son, and Holy Spirit He would in truth be no lonesome, no egotistical God even without man, yes, even without the whole created universe. And He must more than ever be not *for* man; He *could*—one even thinks He *must*— rather be against him. But that is the mystery in which He meets us in the existence of Jesus Christ. He wants in His freedom actually not to be without man but *with* him and in the same freedom not against him but *for* him, and that apart from or even counter to what man deserves. He wants in fact to be man's partner, his almighty and compassionate Saviour.

He chooses to give man the benefit of His power, which encompasses not only the high and the distant but also the deep and the near, in order to maintain communion with him in the realm guaranteed by His deity. He determines to love him, to be his God, his Lord, his compassionate Preserver and Saviour to eternal life, and to desire his praise and service.

In this divinely free volition and election, in this sovereign decision (the ancients said, in His decree), God is *human*. His free affirmation of man, His free concern for him, His free substitution for him—this is God's humanity. We recognize it exactly at the point where we also first recognize His deity. Is it not true that in Jesus Christ, as He is attested in the Holy Scripture, genuine deity includes in itself genuine humanity? There is the father who cares for his lost son, the king who does the same for his insolvent debtor, the Samaritan who takes pity on the one who fell among robbers and in his thoroughgoing act of compassion cares for him in a fashion as unexpected as it is liberal. And this is the act of compassion to which all these parables as parables of the Kingdom of heaven refer. The very One who speaks in these parables takes to His heart the weakness and the perversity, the helplessness and the misery, of the human race surrounding Him. He does not despise men, but in an inconceivable manner esteems them highly just as they are, takes them into His heart and sets Himself in their place. He perceives that the superior will of God, to which He wholly subordinates Himself, requires that He sacrifice Himself for the human race, and seeks His honor in doing this. In the mirror of this humanity of Jesus Christ the humanity of God enclosed in His deity reveals itself. Thus God is as He is. Thus He affirms man. Thus He is concerned about him. Thus He stands up for him. The God of Schleiermacher cannot show mercy. The God of Abraham, Isaac, and Jacob can and does. If Jesus

Christ is the Word of Truth, the "mirror of the fatherly heart of God,"* then Nietzsche's statement that man is something that must be overcome is an impudent lie. Then the truth of God is, as Titus 3:4 says, His loving-kindness and nothing else.

III

We should not yet, however, have arrived at this insight in the right way—in any case we should not yet have been certain of it—if its content had not been evident along the lines which all Christian thinking and speaking must follow. The statement regarding God's humanity, the Immanuel, to which we have advanced as a first step from the Christological center, cannot but have the most far-reaching consequences. These result from the fact that we are asked about the *correspondence*—here the concept of analogy may come into its right—of our thinking and speaking with the humanity of God. The most fundamental and important of these consequences, though not all of them, must now be brought more significantly to light.

From the fact that God is human in the sense described, there follows first of all a quite definite *distinction* of *man* as such. It is a distinction of every being which bears the human countenance. This includes the whole stock of those capacities and possibilities which are in part common to man and to other creatures, and in part peculiar to him, and likewise man's work and his productions. The acknowledgment of this distinction has nothing to do with an optimistic judgment of man. It is due him because he is the being whom God willed to exalt as His covenant-partner, not otherwise. But

---

* Martin Luther.

Hope of God in contra-reality [handwritten annotation]

just because God is human in this sense, it is actually *due* man and may not be denied him through any pessimistic judgment, whatever its basis. On the basis of the eternal will of God we have to think of *every human being*, even the oddest, most villainous or miserable, as one to whom Jesus Christ is Brother and God is Father; and we have to deal with him on this assumption. If the other person knows that already, then we have to strengthen him in the knowledge. If he does not know it yet or no longer knows it, our business is to transmit this knowledge to him. On the basis of the knowledge of the humanity of God no other attitude to any kind of fellow man is possible. It is identical with the practical acknowledgment of his human rights and his human dignity. To deny it to him would be for us to renounce having Jesus Christ as Brother and God as Father.

The distinction due to man as such through the humanity of God, however, extends also to everything with which man as man is endowed and equipped by God, his Creator. This gift, his humanity, is not blotted out through the fall of man, nor is its goodness diminished. Man is not elected to intercourse with God because, by virtue of his humanity, he deserved such preference. He is elected through God's grace alone. He is elected, however, as the being especially endowed by God. This is manifest in his special bodily nature, in which he of course has ever so much in common with plant and animal, and also in the fact that he is a rationally thinking, willing, and speaking being destined for responsible and spontaneous decision. Above all, however, it is shown in the fact that from the beginning he is constituted, bound, and obligated as a fellow man. God concerns Himself with, loves, and calls him as *this* being in his particular totality. In bringing into action his particular nature man, as *this* being, may and should praise Him and be submissive to His grace in thankfulness. It

would not do even partially to cast suspicion upon, under-
value, or speak ill of his humanity, the gift of God, which
characterizes him as this being. We can meet God only within
the limits of humanity determined by Him. But in these limits
we may meet Him. He does not reject the human! Quite the
contrary! We must hold fast to this.

The distinction of man, however, goes still further. It
extends itself indeed even to the particular human activity
based on his endowment, to what one is accustomed to call
human *culture* in its higher and lower levels. Whether as cre-
ators or as beneficiaries of culture, we all participate in it as
persons responsible for it. We *can* exercise no abstinence
toward it, even if we want to. But we should not *want* to do
that. Each of us has his place and his function in its history.
Certainly we must here consider the fact that the use of the
good gift of God and hence human activity with its great and
small results is compromised in the extreme through man's
perverted attitude toward God, toward his neighbor, and
toward himself. Certainly culture testifies clearly in history
and in the present to the fact that man is *not* good but rather
a downright monster. But even if one were in this respect the
most melancholy skeptic, one could not—in view of the
humanity of God which is bestowed upon the man who is not
good or who is even monstrous—say that culture speaks only
of the evil in man. What is culture in itself except the attempt
of man to be man and thus to hold the good gift of his humanity in honor and to put it to work? That in this attempt he
ever and again runs aground and even accomplishes the opposite is a problem in itself, but one which in no way alters
the fact that this attempt is inevitable. Above all, the fact
remains that the *man* who, either as the creator or as the bene-
ficiary, somehow participates in this attempt is the being who
interests God. Finally, it also remains true that God, as Creator

and Lord of man, is always free to produce even in human activity and its results, in spite of the problems involved, *parables* of His own eternal good will and actions. It is more than ever true, then, that with regard to these no proud abstention but only reverence, joy, and gratitude are appropriate.

We must affirm as a second consequence the fact that, through the humanity of God, a quite definite theme is given to *theological* culture in particular. Yes, along with pyramid building, pre- and post-Kantian philosophy, classical poetry, socialism, and theoretical and practical nuclear physics there is also theological culture! Since God in His deity is human, this culture must occupy itself neither with God in Himself nor with man in himself but with the man-encountering God and the God-encountering man and with their dialogue and history, in which their communion takes place and comes to its fulfillment. For this reason theology can think and speak only as it looks at Jesus Christ and from the vantage point of what He is. It cannot introduce Him. Neither can it bring about that dialogue, history, and communion. It does not have the disposition of these things. It is dependent upon the Holy Scripture, according to which the covenant is *in full effect* and in which Jesus Christ *witnesses to Himself*. It hears this witness. It trusts it and is satisfied with it.

Thus through all the centuries theology was, and also today is, given its subject-matter—its theme—and, along with this, instruction in the scholarly and practical objectivity appropriate to it. Theology must hold fast to this objectivity in its exegesis; in its investigation, presentation, and interpretation of the Christian past and present; in its dogmatics and ethics; and in its preaching, instruction, and pastoral ministry. This objectivity means that without allowing itself to be enticed into error, either toward the right or the left, theology will attempt to see, to understand, and to put into language the intercourse of God with man in which there comes about intercourse of man with God. It means that theology will deal with the word and act of the grace of God and the word and act of the human gratitude challenged, awakened, and nourished through it. The first will not be considered without the second nor the second without the first, and both will be approached in the sequence, distinction, and unity given by the deity and thus the humanity of God. When it stays with this theme, it is also in its most modest form good—let us say for once "cultivated"—theology.

Whether the theological existentialism of Rudolf Bultmann and his followers, close to which we find ourselves here, carries us further toward this objectivity which is indispensable to good theology remains yet to be seen. It is not yet clear whether and in what sense a genuine, concrete dialogue, history, and communion between God and man is there envisioned, or whether it is concerned merely with a repristination of the theology of the believing individual who reflects on himself in solitude (this time on his reality and unreality) and explicates himself. The fact that to date neither the people of Israel nor the Christian community appears to have constitutive meaning for this theology causes one concern. And what can be the meaning of the "overcoming of the Subject-Object-Scheme," recently proclaimed with such special enthusiasm, so long as it is not made clear and guaranteed that this enterprise will not once more lead to the anthropocentric myth and call into question anew the *intercourse* between God and man and thus the *object* of theology? Certainly existentialism may have reminded us once again of the elements of truth in the old school by introducing once more the thought that one cannot speak of God without speaking of man. It is to be hoped that it will not lead us back into the old error that one can speak of man without first, and very concretely, having spoken of the living God.

A third consequence: God's humanity and the knowledge of it calls for a definite *attitude* and *alignment* of Christian theological thinking and speaking. It can never approach its subject matter in a vacuum, never in mere theory. Theology cannot fix upon, consider, and put into words any truths which rest on or are moved by themselves—neither an abstract truth about God nor about man nor about the intercourse between God and man. It can never verify, reflect, or report in a monologue. Incidentally, let it be said that there is no theological visual art. Since it is an event, the humanity of God does not permit itself to be fixed in an image.

In conformity with its object, the fundamental form of theology is the prayer and the sermon. It can take only the form of dialogue. Its presupposition and occasion consist in the fact that the commerce between God and man indeed concerns *all men*, in that in Him, namely, in Jesus Christ, the most personal affairs of them all are treated and the life and death of them all are decided. Hence they all must know about Him in order to define their own attitude and to participate in Him. Theology also presupposes that there are many—many too many—who *do not yet* or *no longer* or *do not rightly* know (indeed, in some way all this applies to every man) that it is necessary and imperative to proclaim to men, to call them together, and to communicate. This is your concern! Christian thinking revolves around God's Word of the covenant of peace and likewise around the man who in some way has not, or has not correctly, heard this Word, and to whom it must therefore by all means be proclaimed. And Christian speaking is both prayer to God and an address to this man.

It is *Kerygma*, the herald's call, the message which invites and summons, not to some sort of free-ranging speculation but to special reflection upon faith and obedience, in which man steps out of the mere "interest" of the spectator over into genuine participation* and in which he recognizes his own God in the deity of Jesus Christ as well as himself in His humanity. The exegesis of form criticism has shown us that all this is in the New Testament and that it is normative both for the entire period following the resurrection of Jesus Christ and for that period preceding His direct, universal, and conclusive revelation. In the *Kerygma* man recognizes himself as being under God's judgment and grace, as the receiver of His promise and His command, and thus enters with his own understanding, will, and heart into the reality of that intercourse. Theological thinking and speaking indeed cannot cause this to happen to him. Therefore it cannot have the character of address alone; it must also have the character of prayer. For that reason it can be useful to him and therefore precisely on the basis of this usefulness it must, comformably to the humanity of God Himself, be carried on. Should it not be carried out in this useful way, it would drop not only out of its role but also out of its character; it would betray itself so that, however "Christian" its content might be, it would become profane thinking and speaking.

The question of *language*, about which one must speak in reference to the so-called "outsiders," is not so burning today as is asserted in various quarters. This is true in the first place because, again thinking in terms of the humanity of God, we cannot at all reckon in a serious way with *real* "outsiders," with a "world come of age," but only with a world which

---

* Barth engages in a German-Latin play on words: man steps out of the mere *"Interesse"* . . . into genuine *"Inter-Esse."*

regards itself as of age (and proves daily that it is precisely not that). Thus the so-called "outsiders" are really only "insiders" who have not yet understood and apprehended themselves as such. On the other hand, even the most persuaded Christian, in the final analysis, must and will recognize himself ever and again as an "outsider." So there must then be no particular language for insiders and outsiders. Both are contemporary men-of-the-world—all of us are. A little "non-religious" language from the street, the newspaper, literature, and, if one is ambitious, from the philosopher may thus, for the sake of communication, occasionally indeed be in order. However, we should not become particularly concerned about this. A little of the language of Canaan, a little "revelation-positivism," can also be a good thing in addressing us all and, according to my experience, in which I am certainly not alone, will often, though not always, be still better understood even by the oddest strangers. That is better than feeling compelled to approach them—like a "Jesuit in miniature," certainly no sympathetic figure—with some sort of gibberish, which, for the moment, is modern. What we have to say to them—and first to ourselves—is a strange piece of news in any case. Let us see to it that it really is the *great* piece of news—the message of the eternal love of God directed to us men as we at all times were, are, and shall be. Then we shall certainly be very well understood by them, whatever they may or may not do with it. He whose heart is really with God and therefore really with men may have faith that the Word of God, to which he seeks to bear witness, will not return unto Him void.

A fourth consequence: the *sense* and *sound* of our word must be fundamentally *positive*. Proclamation of the covenant of God with men, announcement of the place which is once for all opened and assigned to man in this covenant, the mes-

sage of Immanuel, the message of Christ—this is the task. The
dialogue and encounter which are our theological theme
involve God's grace and man's gratitude. To open up again
the abyss closed in Jesus Christ cannot be our task. Man is
not good: that is indeed true and must once more be asserted.
God does not turn toward him without uttering in inexorable
sharpness a "No" to his transgression. Thus theology has no
choice but to put this "No" into words within the framework
of its theme. However, it must be the "No" which Jesus Christ
has taken upon Himself for us men, in order that it may no
longer affect us and that we may no longer place ourselves
under it. What takes place in God's humanity is, since it
includes that "No" in itself, the *affirmation* of man.

The direction of our word is given therewith. The man
with whom we have to do in ourselves and in others, although
a rebel, a sluggard, a hypocrite, is likewise the creature to
whom his Creator is faithful and not unfaithful. But there is
still more: he is the being whom God has loved, loves, and will
love, because He has substituted Himself in Jesus Christ and
has made Himself the guarantee. "Jesus is the victor" and
"You men are gods": these two watchwords of Blumhardt
hold good! And with this explanation the statement that the
human spirit is naturally Christian may also be valid as an
obstinately joyful proclamation. That is what we have to
testify to men in view of the humanism *of God*, irrespective
of the more or less dense godlessness of *their* humanism—
everything else must be said only in the framework of this
statement and promise. Thus the bitterest indictments and
the most somber threats of judgment of the Old Testament
prophets are uttered only in the context of the history of the
covenant founded by Yahweh and faithfully preserved despite
all the unfaithfulness of Israel. Thus the Baptist's preaching
of repentance had its basis and meaning only in the Kingdom

of heaven which was already at hand. Thus again certain terrifying passages toward the end of John's Apocalypse find their place and therewith their limits in its final words: "Amen, come Lord Jesus! The grace of the Lord Jesus be with all." The Word of God announced good news to the poor, liberation to the imprisoned, sight to the blind, justification and sanctification and even a call to service to sinners, whether gross or refined. Consider what follows from that: to uncover and expose misunderstandings as such is one thing; to understand and to guide into understanding is another. Hence, moral earnestness is a praiseworthy thing and the gift of penetrating and perhaps witty analysis of the times, of the situation, and of the soul is certainly a fine gift. But the task of bringing the gospel to light is more urgent than manifesting that earnestness and bringing this gift into play. He to whom this *positive* task is not absolutely the supreme task, who first of all wants to shout at, bewilder, or laugh at men on account of their folly and malice, had better remain silent altogether. There is only *one* analogy to the humanity of God in this respect, namely, the message of the great joy—which comforts but in so doing really judges—which is prepared for man by God and which he in turn may have in God. "All my springs are in you!" (Psalm 87:7.)

Does this mean universalism? I wish here to make only three short observations, in which one is to detect no position for or against that which passes among us under this term.

1. One should not surrender himself in any case to the panic which this word seems to spread abroad, before informing himself exactly concerning its possible sense or non-sense.

2. One should at least be stimulated by the passage, Colossians 1:19, which admittedly states that God has determined through His Son as His image and as the first-born of the whole Creation to "reconcile all things (τὰ πάντα) to himself,"

to consider whether the concept could not perhaps have a good meaning. The same can be said of parallel passages.

3. One question should for a moment be asked, in view of the "danger" with which one may see this concept gradually surrounded. What of the "danger" of the eternally skeptical-critical theologian who is ever and again suspiciously questioning, because fundamentally always legalistic and therefore in the main morosely gloomy? Is not his presence among us currently more threatening than that of the unbecomingly cheerful indifferentism or even antinomianism, to which one with a certain understanding of universalism could in fact deliver himself? This much is certain, that we have no theological right to set any sort of limits to the loving-kindness of God which has appeared in Jesus Christ. Our theological duty is to see and understand it as being still greater than we had seen before.

And now in conclusion still a fifth consequence: in the knowledge of the humanity of God one must take seriously, affirm, and thankfully acknowledge *Christendom*, the *Church*. We must, each in his place, take part in its life and join in its service. It was a part of the exaggerations of which we were guilty in 1920 that we were able to see the theological relevance of the Church only as a negative counterpart to the Kingdom of God which we had then so happily rediscovered. We wanted to interpret the form of the Church's doctrine, its worship, its juridical order as "human, all too human," as "not so important." We regarded all the earnestness or even zeal devoted to them as superfluous or even injurious. In all this we at least approached the theory and practice of a spiritual partisanship and an esoteric gnosticism.

It is now, in view of the actual and recurrent Roman temptation, certainly not appropriate to silence or even to soften the stress on the judgment beginning with the house of God which, after all, runs through the entire Bible. It is likewise inappropriate, in view of the ecclesiastical, confessional, and on the whole traditional—even clerical and liturgical—restoration and reaction current in present-day Germany, which perhaps one day may encroach upon our land. And it certainly was and is no good undertaking to reverse the sequence whereby *event* precedes *institution,* which is also established by the entire Bible. We had and still have to see and to understand, however, that the maintenance of this sequence and the remembrance of that judgment must in no case result in neglect or renunciation of our solidarity with the Church. The word which is critical of the Church can be meaningful and fruitful only when it stems from insight—I do not say too much—into the existence and function of the Church as necessary for salvation. It must be spoken with the intention of serving her in her gathering together, her edification and mission. The humanity of God is relevant to the old and the new Israel, to the individual man who exists in his own place and not in some sort of vacuum. Jesus Christ is the Head of His body and only so is He also the Head of its members. The acknowledgment of God's work accomplished in Him implies that it has taken place for *us* and thus only in this way for *me.* The Lord's Prayer is a *we*-prayer and only in this way also an *I*-prayer. "We" are the Church. The Church is the particular people, the congregation, or in Calvin's term, the company, which through a bit of knowledge of the gracious God manifest in Jesus Christ is constituted, appointed, and called as His witness in the world. This knowledge is paltry indeed, but because it is established by the Holy Spirit, it is unconquerable.

What is the existence of this particular people but the reflection of the humanity of God, although it is admittedly everywhere blurred and darkened and in its continuity all too often interrupted? This turning of God to man calls out and awakens some to worship, praise, and serve Him—many of them for the time being as representative of others and as His messengers to them. We should be inhuman where God is human, we should be ashamed of Jesus Christ Himself, were we willing to be ashamed of the Church. What Jesus Christ is for God and for us, on earth and in time, He is as Lord of this community, as King of this people, as Head of this body and of all its members. He is all these with and in this inconspicuous, painfully divided, and otherwise very questionable Christendom. He is all these with, among, and in the Christians whom one can admire or even love only in the face of many serious difficulties. He is all these as the Reconciler and Redeemer of the whole world. He is all these, however, in the strange communion of these strange saints. The Church is not too mean a thing for Him but, for better or for worse, sufficiently precious and worthy in His eyes to be entrusted with His witnessing and thus His affairs in the world—yes, even Himself. So great is God's loving-kindness!

For this reason there is no private Christianity. For this reason we cannot but take seriously, affirm, and love this community in its peculiarity. While we cannot but view critically in all details its assuredly human—all too human— efforts for better knowledge and better confession, for its meetings, its inner order, and its outward task, we must also view them as seriously important. For this reason, too, theology cannot be carried on in the private lighthouses of some sort of merely personal discoveries and opinions. It can be carried on only in the Church—it can be put to work in all its elements only in the context of the questioning and answering of the Christian community and in the rigorous service of its commission to all men. One must perhaps himself have had a part in the life of the Church during a difficult period to know that there are hours in its work, its struggle, and its suffering in which not less than everything can depend upon some human, very human, iota or dot in its decisions and also in its thinking and speaking. One will then approach more cautiously the mood in which one sees only inconsequential matters in the Church. In a really living Church there is perhaps nothing inconsequential at all.

But however that may be, our "I believe in the Holy Spirit" would be empty if it did not also include in a concrete, practical, and obligatory way the "I believe one Holy Catholic and Apostolic Church." We believe the Church as the place where the crown of humanity, namely, man's fellow-humanity, may become visible in Christocratic brotherhood. Moreover, we believe it as the place where God's glory wills to dwell upon earth, that is, where humanity—the humanity of God—wills to assume tangible form in time and here upon earth. Here we recognize the humanity of God. Here we delight in it. Here we celebrate and witness to it. Here we glory in the Immanuel, just as He did who, as He looked at the world, would not cast away the burden of the Church but rather chose to take it upon Himself and bear it in the name of all its members. "If God is for us, who is against us?"

THE GIFT OF FREEDOM
FOUNDATION OF EVANGELICAL ETHICS

THE GIFT OF FREEDOM
FOUNDATION OF EVANGELICAL ETHICS*

It is my task to discuss the gift of freedom, and to do so with the foundation of evangelical ethics in view. Let me anticipate the solution to the problem inherent in this theme in three summary propositions. The first describes the freedom which *God* Himself possesses; the second delineates it as the gift bestowed by God upon *man;* the third relates the consequences of these two to the problem of the foundation of evangelical *ethics.*

First: *God's freedom is His very own.* It is the sovereign grace wherein God chooses to commit Himself to man. Thereby God is Lord as *man's* God.

Secondly: *Man's freedom is his as the gift of God.* It is the joy wherein man appropriates God's election. Thereby man is God's creature, His partner, and His child as *God's* man.

Thirdly: Evangelical ethics is the reflection upon the *divine call to human action* which is implied by the gift of freedom.

I

We begin by examining what man may know about *God's own freedom.* Must I justify my starting with God's own freedom rather than with anything else? Must I justify my not beginning with man's innate or given freedom? I, too, have heard the news that we can speak about *God* only by speaking about *man.* I do not contest this claim. Rightly interpreted,

* Address given at a meeting of the *Gesellschaft für Evangelische Theologie,* Bielefeld, September 21, 1953.

If Humanity of God

it may be an expression of the true insight that God is not without man. This means in our particular context that God's own freedom must be recognized as freedom to be a partisan for man.

We may not speak of God's own freedom apart from the history of God's dealings with man. Man's God-given freedom, then, must be acknowledged from the very beginning. But this claim, correctly understood, calls for a counterclaim. We can speak about man only by speaking about God. This general statement is hardly disputed among Christian theologians. There is, however, sharp disagreement as to the priority of the two claims. It is my firm conviction that what I have just called the counterclaim is the true claim and must come first. Why deny priority to God in the realm of knowing when it is uncontested in the realm of being? If God is the first reality, how can man be the first truth?

Those holding the opposite view go so far as to say that the God-given freedom of man is, first of all, freedom of man from himself. But how does this bold statement prompt man to begin as a thinker with himself as a starting point? Why, of all concepts in Christian theology, should the concept of God merely have the function of a boundary term? Why should it connote only a vacuum to be filled at best with subsequent and nonessential assertions about the ideal or historical conditions of human existence? Is it so self-evident that man is intimately known to us, whereas God remains the great and doubtful Unknown? Is it, then, a law of the Medes and the Persians that our quest for God must proceed on the basis of our supposed knowledge of man? Does not this freedom, bestowed by God upon man and, as we shall discuss later, specifically upon the Christian theologian, prompt man to overcome this mental block and to think in a new perspective, to think even exclusively in a new perspective? Is not this new perspective mapped out for man in God's revelation, showing forth first and foremost God Himself, and in this way and only then revealing man to himself? Where else can we learn that freedom exists and what it is, except in confrontation with God's own freedom offered to us as the source and measure of all freedom? We do not speculate beyond man nor do we abandon him and his freedom by first inquiring about the One who is man's *God* and about His own freedom. On the contrary, we then may seek and find true man and his true freedom.

God's freedom is not merely unlimited possibility or formal majesty and omnipotence, that is to say empty, naked sovereignty. Nor is this true of the God-given freedom of man. If we so misinterpret human freedom, it irreconcilably clashes with divine freedom and becomes the false freedom of sin, reducing man to a prisoner. God Himself, if conceived of as unconditioned power, would be a demon and as such His own prisoner. In the light of His revelation, God is free in word and deed; He is the source and measure of all freedom, insofar as He is the Lord, choosing and determining Himself first of all. In His own freedom, as the source of human freedom, God above all willed and determined Himself to be the Father and the Son in the unity of the Spirit. This is not abstract freedom. Nor is it the freedom of aloof isolation. Likewise, man's God-given freedom is not to be sought and found in any solitary detachment from God. In God's own freedom there is encounter and communion; there is order and, consequently, dominion and subordination; there is majesty and humility, absolute authority and absolute obedience; there is offer and response.

God's freedom is the freedom of the Father and the Son in the unity of the Spirit. Again, man's freedom is a far cry from the self-assertion of one or many solitary individuals. It has nothing to do with division and disorder. God's own freedom is trinitarian, embracing grace, thankfulness, and peace. It is the freedom of the living God. Only in this relational freedom is God sovereign, almighty, the Lord of all.

In this freedom God is, again according to His revelation, *man's* God. To put it more concretely: He is the God of Abraham, Isaac, and Jacob. He is man's God not because man projected, patterned, and exalted Him, not because Israel chose Him, but because He chose, decided, and determined Himself for His Israel and with Israel for mankind. The well-known definitions of the essence of God and in particular of His freedom, containing such terms as "wholly other," "transcendence," or "non-worldly," stand in need of thorough clarification if fatal misconceptions of human freedom as well are to be avoided. The above definitions might just as well fit a dead idol. Negative as they are, they most certainly miss the very center of the Christian concept of God, the radiant affirmation of free grace, whereby God bound and committed Himself to man, making Himself in His Son a man of Israel and the brother of all men, appropriating human nature into the unity of His own being. If this is true, if this is not an accidental historical fact but in its historical uniqueness is the revelation of the divine will, valid and powerful before, above, after, and in all history, then God's freedom is essentially not freedom *from,* but freedom *to* and *for.* (We shall have to remember this point in our discussion of human freedom.) God is free for *man,* free to coexist with man and, as the Lord of the covenant, to participate in his *history.* The concept of God without man is indeed as anomalous as wooden iron.

In His free grace, God is for man in every respect; He surrounds man from all sides. He is man's Lord who is before him, above him, after him, and thence also with him in history, the locus of man's existence. Despite man's insignificance,

God is with him as his Creator who intended and made mankind to be very good. Despite man's sin, God is with him, the
One who was in Jesus Christ reconciling the world, drawing
man unto Himself in merciful judgment. Man's evil past is not
merely crossed out because of its irrelevancy. Rather, it is in the
good care of God. Despite man's life in the flesh, corrupt and
ephemeral, God is with him. The victor in Christ is here and
now present through His Spirit, man's strength, companion,
and comfort. Despite man's death God is with him, meeting
him as redeemer and perfecter at the threshold of the future
to show him the totality of existence in the true light in which
the eyes of God beheld it from the beginning and will behold
it evermore. In what He is for man and does for man, God
ushers in the history leading to the ultimate salvation of man.

   Though in a different way, God is beyond doubt also before, above, after, and with all of His other creatures. However, we may at best venture some ideas of this difference in
the meaning of God's freedom for these creatures, of the gift
of freedom to them. In reality we have no precise knowledge
about this. Through His revelation God is known in His
loving-kindness to us as the God of man. However, God was
not and is not bound to choose and to decide Himself for man
alone and to show His loving-kindness to him alone. The
thought of any insignificant being outside the human cosmos
being far more worthy of divine attention than man is deeply
edifying and should not be lightly dismissed. But it remains
true that God who gave His Son to become and to remain our
brother assures us that He willed to love *man*, that He loved
us and still loves us and shall love us because He chose and
determined Himself to be our God.

   This freedom of God as it is expressed in His being, word,
and deed is the content of the *Gospel*. Receiving this good
news from those who witness to it, the Christian *community*

in the world is called to acknowledge it in faith, to respond to it in love, to set on it its hope and trust, and to proclaim it to the world which belongs to this free God. It is the privilege and the mission of the Christian community to acknowledge and to confess the Gospel. By acknowledging and confessing Jesus Christ as the creation and revelation of God's freedom, this community is incorporated into the body of Christ and becomes the earthly and historical form of His existence. He is in its midst.

We do well to keep remembering that the existence of the Christian community, through its preaching and its works, is already an expression of man's God-given freedom. Let us therefore respect the difference in perspective! The existence of the Christian community in its faith, love, and hope, and in its proclamation, is unmistakably part of the divinely inaugurated *Heilsgeschichte*. It is part of it insofar as to acknowledge and confess God's freedom is an act of the freedom bestowed upon man in the course of this history. But it is and remains an act of human freedom. The divine freedom was not initiated in and by this act of human freedom. Nor is it accomplished and somehow encompassed in it. Rather, God's freedom is and remains above and beyond human freedom. Measured against the act of divine freedom, the act of human freedom has its own beginning, its own course, and its own preliminary and relative ends. None of these coincide or are to be confounded with those of the *Heilsgeschichte*. It remains the prerogative of the divine freedom to set the end of this history, the beginning of which it set also.

God's own freedom and its realizations is the source and object of every Christian act of recognition and confession. It is sufficient that this human act takes place in the context of the freedom of God to which it bears witness. Yahweh lives and will live in solidarity, but not in identity, with Israel. The same holds true for Jesus Christ, the word and deed of God, with regard to His community, to the task it has to perform in response to the gift of freedom, and to its *kerygma*. The head does not become the body and the body does not become the head. The king does not become his own messenger, and the messenger does not become king. It is sufficient that the community be called into being, be created, protected, and sustained by Jesus Christ, and that it may confess Him who came into the world, is present now, and shall come in glory. It may confess Him who was, is, and shall be the word and deed of God's freedom and of His all-embracing loving-kindness.

II

God in His own freedom bestows human freedom. Here we must point to so-called *natural* freedom which constitutes and characterizes human existence in its creatureliness, and to the freedom of eternal life *promised* to man. Here, for once, we must daringly include both in what is to be said about *Christian* freedom. Christian freedom is divinely bestowed upon man despite his sin, despite his existence in the flesh, and despite his being threatened by death. "Natural freedom" and "freedom promised" must, in any event, be understood on the basis of "Christian freedom." This is because freedom is made known to us by God as the "freedom of the Christian man." Human freedom is the *gift of God in the free outpouring* of His grace. To call a man free is to recognize that God has *given* him freedom. Human freedom is enacted within history, that history which leads to the ultimate salvation of man. Human freedom never ceases to be the event wherein the free God gives and man receives this gift. God freely makes Himself available to man by granting him the freedom he is meant to have. Whatever the subsequent events of this history may

be, they take place within the context and under the judgment
of this divine act of mercy. Seen from the vantage point of
the free gift of the free God, the concept of unfree man is a
contradiction in itself. Unfree man is a creature of chaos, a
monster begotten by his own pride, his own laziness, his own
lies.

The concept of freedom as man's rightful claim and due is
equally contradictory and impossible. So is the thought of
man's acquiring freedom by earning it or buying it at any
price. The idea that man can conquer freedom as God's antag-
onist and defiantly wrench it from Him is untenable. Man has
no real will power. Nor does he get it by himself. His power
lies in receiving and in appropriating God's gift. The event of
man's freedom is the event of his thankfulness for the gift,
of his sense of responsibility as a receiver, of his loving care for
what is given him. It is his reverence before the free God
who accepts him as His partner without relinquishing His
sovereignty. This event alone is the event of freedom.

The gift of freedom, however, involves more than being
offered one option among several. It involves more than being
asked a question, being presented with an opportunity, and
having a possibility opened up. The gift is total, unequivocal,
and irrevocable. It remains the gift of freedom even though it
may be turned into man's judgment if misunderstood or mis-
used. We are dealing with the gift of the free God. God does
not put man into the situation of Hercules at the crossroads.
The opposite is true. God frees man from this false situation.
He lifts him from appearance to reality. It is true that man's
God-given freedom is choice, decision, act. But it is genuine
choice; it is genuine decision and act in the right direction.

It would be a strange freedom that would leave man neutral,
able equally to choose, decide, and act rightly or wrongly!
What kind of power would that be! Man becomes free and

is free by choosing, deciding, and determining himself in accordance with the freedom of God. The source of man's freedom is also its yardstick. Trying to escape from being in accord with God's own freedom is not human freedom. Rather, it is a compulsion wrought by powers of darkness or by man's own helplessness. Sin as an alternative is not anticipated or included in the freedom given to man by God. Nor can sin be explained and theoretically justified by this freedom. No excuse can be provided for sin. In human freedom there is no room for sin by fiat. Sinful man is not free, he is a captive, a slave. When genuine human freedom is realized, inevitably the door to the "right" opens and the door to the "left" is shut. This inevitability is what makes God's gift of freedom so marvelous, and yet at the same time so terrifying.

As a gift of God, human freedom cannot contradict divine freedom. This leads to certain limitations regarding human freedom which are similar to those mentioned in our earlier attempt to define the freedom of God. We now make bold to say:

(1) Human freedom as a gift of God does not allow for any vague choices between various possibilities. The reign of chance and ambiguity is excluded. For the free God Himself, the giver of man's freedom, is no blind accident, no tyrant. He is the Lord, choosing and determining Himself unmistakably once and for all. He is His own law.

(2) Human freedom is not realized in the solitary detachment of an individual in isolation from his fellow men. God is *a se* (for Himself), but He is *pro nobis* (for us). For us! It is true that He who gave man freedom because He is man's friend, is also *pro me* (for me). But I am not Man, I am only *a man*, and I am a man only in relation to my fellow men. Only in encounter and in communion with them may I receive the gift of freedom. God is *pro me* because He is *pro nobis*.

(3) Human freedom is only secondarily freedom *from* limitations and threats. Primarily it is freedom *for*.

(4) Human freedom is not to be understood as freedom to assert, to preserve, to justify and save oneself. God is primarily free *for;* the Father is free for the Son, the Son for the Father in the unity of the Spirit. The one God is free for man as his Creator, as the Lord of the covenant, as the beginner and perfecter of his history, his *Heilsgeschichte*. God says "Yes." Only once this "Yes" is said, He also says "No." Thereby He reveals Himself to be *free from* all that is alien and hostile to His nature. Only once this "Yes" is said, is He free for Himself and for His own glory. Human freedom is freedom only within the limitations of God's own freedom.

And thus we can see that freedom is *being joyful*. Freedom is the great gift, totally unmerited and wondrous beyond understanding. It awakens the receiver to true selfhood and new life. It is a gift from *God*, from the source of all goodness, an ever-new token of His faithfulness and mercy. The gift is unambiguous and cannot fail. Through this gift man who was irretrievably separated and alienated from God is called into discipleship. This is why freedom is joy! Certainly, man does not live up to this freedom. Even worse, he fails in every respect. It is true enough that he does not know any longer the natural freedom which was bestowed upon him in creation; he does not know as yet the ultimate freedom in store for him at the completion of his journey, in the ultimate fulfillment of his existence. It is true enough that man may presently know and enjoy this freedom through the abiding Spirit of the Father and the Son only in spite of sin, flesh, and death; in spite of the world, his earthly anxiety and his worldly nature; and in spite of himself in his persistent temptation. This however, does not prevent man from being enabled to know and to live out this freedom in incomparable and inexhaustible joy, limited as his own awareness may be. Some may not want any part of it, and at times we all feel this way. But this does not change anything. God's gift is there for all. It is poured out at the beginning of our journey, at its destination, and most certainly also in our present plight. Freedom is waiting here and now to be received and lived out in joy, albeit a joy that is not without travail.

Human freedom is the joy whereby man appropriates for himself God's election. God has elected Himself in His Son to be the God, Lord, Shepherd, Saviour, and Redeemer of mankind. Through His own election He willed man to be His creature, His partner, and His son. He, the God of the community of men, and we, the community of men, His people! Freedom is the joy whereby man acknowledges and confesses this divine election by willing, deciding, and determining himself to be the echo and mirror of the divine act. Each individual is called to this commitment in the midst of the community of men, not as the first disciple but as a follower in the visible and invisible footsteps of many; not as the only one but together with many known and unknown fellow Christians. He may be accompanied by the comforting help of several or by at least a few. He may be a rather sad member of the rear guard or he may be way ahead of the crowd where he is temporarily alone. He lives for himself, but not only for himself. He is constantly in living relationship to others, as a member of the people of God who appropriates for himself God's election and is responsible for the brothers. Each individual is called by his own name as a member of the people of God. Each one is responsible for his relationship with God and his fellow men. He is free because he chooses, decides, and determines himself to be this person. His freedom is the joy of that obedience which is given to him. This is a daring venture whenever it is undertaken. A venture at one's own risk and peril? Never! It is the venture of responsibility in the presence of the Giver and the fellow receivers of the gift—past, present, and future. It is the venture of obedience whereby man reflects in his own life God's offer and his own response. This is the life of obedience, allowed for by man's freedom: to will himself to be that member of God's household which God willed him to be.

Free man wills himself to be God's *creature* according to that distinctive structure and limitation of his human nature which sets man apart from all other beings. God wants man free together with his fellow men in the greatness and the misery, in the promise and the anxiety, in the richness and the poverty of his humanity. True enough, man no longer knows what it means to be truly human. Alienated from God, he is alienated from himself and from his true nature. But God does not cease to call and to claim this estranged creature for His own. Likewise, man does not cease to be called and claimed by God as this estranged creature. The gift of freedom makes man free to be not more and not less than human. Whatever God's other intentions for man may be, they will always be a confirmation of his nature as a creature of God. And whatever man may choose to do with his God-given freedom, it always will have to be carried out within the framework of human possibilities. If he cannot boast of his human condition and achievement because they are a gift of God, he need not be ashamed of them either. God does not expect extraordinary accomplishments nor does he expect a jaded or lazy response. He does, however, expect man to realize in his life the divine intention of true humanity inherent in the gift. Glorifying God and loving his neighbor are sure signs of man's commitment.

God wants man to be His creature. Furthermore, He wants him to be His *partner*. There is a *causa Dei* in the world. God wants light, not darkness. He wants cosmos, not chaos. He wants peace, not disorder. He wants man to administer and to receive justice rather than to inflict and to suffer injustice. He wants man to live according to the Spirit rather than according to the flesh. He wants man bound and pledged to Him rather than to any other authority. He wants man to live and not to die. Because He wills these things God is Lord, Shepherd, and Redeemer of man, who in His holiness and mercy meets His creature; who judges and forgives, rejects and receives, condemns and saves. This is not the place to describe the divine act of reconciliation even in its main outline. It is enough to say that God's "Yes" and "No," spoken in His act of reconciliation, is not proclaimed apart from man. Even in this central act God declines to be alone, without man. God insists on man's participation in His reconciling work. He wants man, not as a secondary God, to be sure, but as a truly free follower and co-worker, to repeat His divine "Yes" and "No." This is the meaning of God's covenant with man. This is the task man is called to fulfill when God enters into the covenant relationship with him. This is the freedom of discipleship bestowed upon him.

The sovereign God alone saved man from the alienation and depravity of which he was and still is guilty. He delivered him from the imprisonment and slavery which was and still is his human lot. In the death of Jesus Christ, perfect reconciliation, beyond any need for improvement or repetition, took place once and for all. In His resurrection, and nowhere else, as long as time lasts, God's act of reconciliation is unmistakably revealed. There is no need whatsoever for this divine act to be re-enacted by man in order to be efficacious. This is not to say, however, that man is confined to the role of an approving spectator. The gift of freedom becomes operative at this critical point. Man's freedom always remains human freedom and

is not to be confused with the divine freedom whereby God
in Jesus Christ took man's part.

Human freedom is the God-given freedom to obey. *Faith is*
the obedience of the *pilgrim* who has his vision and his trust
set upon God's free act of reconciliation. This obedience con-
firms and evinces the transition from sin to righteousness, from
the flesh to the spirit, from the law to the sovereignty of the
living God, from death to life in the small and preliminary,
yet determined, steps of the daily journey. *Love* is the obedience of the *witness* who is summoned to announce this transition. The witness announces God's victorious deed, offered
to all his brothers and sisters far and nigh so that they might
greet it as their light. This obedience in love and faith is the
human response to the divine offer of justification, sanctification, and calling in Jesus Christ.

Thus human freedom is freedom to respond with thanksgiving. It is the *freedom of the Christian man* whom God
chooses to be His partner and whom He does not abandon.
God does not expect from man more than this gratitude, this
faith, and this love. Nor does He expect less, and He certainly
expects nothing else! For this service of thankful obedience,
for this participation in the *causa Dei,* God has set man free.

God wants man to be His creature and His partner. Even
more, He wants him to be His *child.* God is not content with
man living as a reverent creature *before* Him, or as a grateful
partner *alongside* Him. He wants him to be a man *with* Him,
and to enjoy the glorious assurance of belonging to God. This
assurance points to man's future, his eternal life. But man as he
is here and now, cannot see himself enjoying this eternal relationship. He cannot understand himself in this dimension,
not even in faith and love. Man bestowed with eternal life is
future man; he is the object of God's promise and of our hope.
And yet he is not devoid of reality. In God's free deed, in

Jesus Christ, man *is* God's child. But as long as man lives he remains a pilgrim and a witness. He can only call on God from afar and out of the depth, *"Our Father who art in heaven!"* He does not yet understand himself as the child who enjoys the glorious assurance of belonging to the Father. For as yet he is an enigma to himself, and his brothers and sisters in the Christian community are enigmas to him as well. As yet his eternal destination is hidden and not revealed.

Even though man as he is here and now does not see or understand himself as a child of God, the God-given freedom breaks through in a new dimension, in a decisive and definitive way. Man is free to call God "Our Father" here and now. Man is free to see things from the standpoint of the beginning, the revealed act of the free God in the here and now. He can see his end in the ultimate revelation of God's act, his belonging to Him in glory. Frustrated, yet comforted in the midst of frustration, he will steadfastly look to the end. Human freedom is to live, to suffer, and finally to die in this expectation. But before he dies, as long as the day lasts, man is free to work, to rise after each fall, to labor and not to grow weary. Whether or not we rise or tire depends on the use we make of our freedom to look to the end. "Jesus, give me eyes, and touch my eyes that they may serve,"* says a well-known hymn. Man is free to bring his plea before God. In so doing he is free to hope for the great light, the great vision that will illumine the world, the Church, his fellow man, and himself. A Christian is one who makes use of this freedom to pray and to live in the hope of the end which will be the revelation of the beginning.

III

We now turn to the question of what these assumptions

* "Jesus, gib gesunde Augen, die was taugen, rühre meine Augen an."

may teach us about the foundation of *evangelical ethics*. Although we cannot elaborate on these foundations at this point, we can at least give an outline.*

A free man is one who chooses, decides, and determines himself and who acts according to his thoughts, words, and deeds. The course of his actions is a consequence of the nature of his God-given freedom. It is therefore in order to use interchangeably freedom and commandment. Man does the good when he acts according to the imperative inherent in the gift of freedom. He does the evil when he obeys a law that is contrary to his freedom. But these definitions need to be qualified.

Man's freedom as the directive and criterion for his actions is the gift bestowed upon him in a historical event of the free God's encounter with him. The giver does not retreat behind his gift, nor the lawmaker behind the law, nor divine freedom behind human freedom. It is God who determines how human freedom becomes directive and criterion for human action. Free man is subject to God's most concrete command, for through this command human freedom takes on authoritative form and the imperative whereby man is confronted and measured becomes decisive. God is always man's Creator, Reconciler, and Redeemer. He wants man to be His creature, His partner, and His child. What this means for each of us here and there, today and tomorrow, is decided by the free word of the free Lord in ever-renewed encounter between God and an individual. Measured against the divine commandment, man's action—his ethos—is found either good or evil. If our interpretation of divine and human freedom is accepted, these terms affirm the content and consequence of the impera-

---

* Those interested in a more detailed description may consult *Church Dogmatics*, I, 2 (par. 22, sec. 3), II, 2 (par. 36-39), III, 4.

tive and the criterion, and concurrently exclude any arbitrary
and accidental characteristics.

Ethics must be understood as the attempt, scientific or otherwise, to cope with the question of good and evil in human
behavior.

Ethics according to our assumptions can only be *evangelical ethics*. The question of good and evil is never answered by
man's pointing to the authoritative Word of God in terms of
a set of rules. It is never discovered by man or imposed on the
self and others as a code of good and evil actions, a sort of yardstick of what is good and evil. Holy Scripture defies being
forced into a set of rules; it is a mistake to use it as such.
The ethicist cannot take the place either of the free God or of
free man, even less of both together. His prescriptions in no
way prejudge either the divine imperative or human obedience. On what authority would he prescribe, even though he
quoted Bible verses, what a certain human being at a certain
time should do or not do? Any such pretense, though well
intended, is bound to lead astray. When the divine imperative
urges upon man here and now a decision on a course of action, in harmony with the will of God, the ethicist will fail
man with even his most realistic prescriptions and leave him
utterly alone. Alas, he will be left alone not with God, but
rather with himself, with his own conscience, with the *kairos*,
or with his own judgment. In this realistic situation the choice
between good and evil is made. To offer ethical norms to man
in this predicament is to hold out a stone instead of bread.

If only ethics could reveal to man from the very beginning
that in wrestling with the problem of his good or evil actions
he is not confronted with his conscience, with the *kairos*, with
his own judgment, with any visible or invisible law of nature
or history, with any individual or social ideals, and, least of
all, with his own arbitrary will. If only ethics could tell him

that as a free man he is confronted with the will, word, and deed of the free God!

Ethics is a *theory* of human behavior. This does not speak against the necessary ethical task. It merely emphasizes that the ethical theory is not meant to provide man with a program the implementation of which would be his life's goal. Nor is it meant to present man with principles to be interpreted, applied, and put into practice. Ethics has to make clear that every single step man takes involves a specific and direct responsibility toward God, who reached out for man in specific and direct encounter. This responsibility is lived out in obedience or disobedience, in good or evil, in confirmation or in negation and loss of the gift of freedom. Ethics exists to remind man of his confrontation with God, who is the light illuminating all his actions. It must be man's guide in his discernment of the apparently unlimited possibilities and in his choice of the only true one, existing either now or in the future. It must be man's teacher of evangelical ethics as the ethics of free grace.

Evangelical ethics will leave the pronouncement of unconditional imperatives to God. Its task is to emphasize the reality and the conditioning of human life, lived in the light of the divine imperative. This does not exclude the possibility of conditional imperatives addressed in concrete situations by a person to a brother. It is part of the risk of obedience involved in the encounter and communion between Christian brothers, and it is part of the risk of action according to the God-given freedom, to be called to invite, even to urge, a brother to a concrete action in a concrete situation, and to ask from him a concrete decision. Man will do so with his eyes lifted up to the living God who is also his brother's God. He will do so with his mind set on human freedom given to his brother also. If his courage is nourished by humility before God and his

fellow men, this attitude alone may justify such conditional
advice. He who takes the risk of counseling must be prepared
to be counseled in turn by his brother if there is need of it.
Such mutual counseling in a concrete situation is an event. It
is part of the ethos which is realized ethics. It is only indirectly
or not at all a part of ethics proper. For ethics is theory and
not practice, though it is the theory about practice. Its main
problem is precisely the question of the ethos, of the right and
wrong, in human action. The ethos of the ethicist implies
that he refrain from attempting too much and becoming
thereby a lawmaker.

Ethics is reflection upon what man is required to do in and
with the gift of freedom. The ethicist should not want to
attempt too little either. He must want to realize his calling
and his talents. It is not enough to insist that human life is to
be lived under the divine imperative. Ethical reflection must
go further and ask the question to what extent this is so.
Neither the freedom of God's commandment nor that of
man's obedience is empty form. Human action takes place
at the point of contact between these two spheres of freedom.
Each of these is characterized by its own content, tone, and
extent. Ethical reflection has to concentrate upon these. It has
to begin with the recognition that the free God is the free
man's Lord, Creator, Reconciler, and Redeemer, and that free
man is God's creature, partner, and child. This insight will be
gained at the very source of Christian thinking, in Holy
Scripture, where ethical reflection will also renew, sharpen,
and correct its findings in continuous searching. In addition,
ethical reflection may and must consult the Christian community in its past and present history. It must do this in order
to be admonished, nourished, enriched, perhaps also stirred
and warned, by the use which the fathers and brethren made
and still are making of Christian freedom.

Therefore, ethics is not without signposts in its attempt to point to God's authoritative word of judgment. If it is based on the knowledge of God and of man, it will receive its contour. It will not point to a vacuum, but to the true God, the real man, and the real encounter between them. The ethical quest is and remains a quest and yet is not totally devoid of fulfillment. Indirect as it may be, the quest is a witness to God's concrete word. Ethical reflection may and must be genuine search and genuine doctrine, genuine because true ethics does not deprive God, its object, of His due power and glory. It leaves the uttering of the essential and final word to God Himself. But it does not shrink away from the preliminary words which are necessary to focus man's wandering thoughts on the one center where he, himself free, shall hear the word of the free God, the commandment addressed to him, the judgment falling upon him, and the promise waiting for him.

IV

These short and general comments on the foundation of evangelical ethics may suffice. Our discussion afterwards might well center on the above remarks, so as not to get sidetracked from the central theme by the additional, and perhaps distracting, remarks I would now like to make. Indeed, before concluding, I propose a short excursion into the field of ethics proper, of what we call "special ethics." I shall take as my starting point the above-described presuppositions. Other speakers will lead you during the next few days to the main points of interest in this vast field. We are gathered here under the auspices of the "Gesellschaft für evangelische Theologie" (Society for Evangelical Theology). This is why I shall choose, as an example and merely as an example, a small and often neglected area: the ethics of theology itself and the ethos of the free theologian.

Is not the free theologian also a man and as such a recipient of the gift of freedom? Does not God address him, his thinking, speaking, and acting as well, when He gives man His commandment in and with the gift of freedom? Let it be noted that according to truly evangelical teaching the term "theologian" is not confined to the seminary professor, to the theological student, or to the minister. It is meant for every Christian who is mindful of the theological task entrusted to the whole Christian congregation, and who is willing and able to share in the common endeavor according to his own talents. We are about to call it a day and are rather tired. I may, therefore, be excused for substituting some isolated remarks for a systematic development of the problem. And because I belong to the old guard today, I may be allowed to switch, at least in feeling tone, from ethics to a sort of admonition. You may be assured that there will be no deviations into imperatives of any kind.

(1) A free theologian, free according to our definition, will be found ready, willing, and able always to begin his thinking *at the beginning*. This means his recognition of the resurrection of Jesus Christ as the directive for his reasoning. In his reflections and statements he will always first proceed from God's relationship to man and only then continue with man's relationship to God. There is an abundance of serious, pious, learned, and ingenious theological undertaking. But lacking the sky-light and hence serenity, the theologian remains a gloomy visitor upon this earth of darkness, an unpleasant instructor of his brethren, whose teaching, at best, compares with the somber music of Beethoven and Brahms! The thoughtful theologian who refuses to begin with God is bound to begin with misery, individual and corporate, with the chaos

which threatens him and the world around him, with anxieties and problems. He will turn around in circles and end up
precisely where he started. Cut off from the fresh air, he
considers it to be his bounden duty not to let others breathe
fresh air either. Only the radical turnabout we have been
advocating here could rescue him. Nobody has accomplished
this turnabout once and forever. Man has been set free for this
very event, this act of obedience which calls for repetition
every day, every hour, whenever a new theological task presents itself. There is no reason for complaint about the impossibility of such a turnabout. True, this turnabout is not a
dialectical trick to be learned and then used merrily again and
again. Without the invocation, "Our Father, who art in
heaven!" this turnabout cannot take place. This is why it is
imperative to recognize the essence of theology as lying in
the liturgical action of adoration, thanksgiving, and petition.
The old saying, *Lex orandi lex credendi*, far from being a
pious statement, is one of the most profound descriptions of
the theological method. We cannot do without this turnabout.
The free and true theologian lives from it. In the invocation, in
the giving of thanks, and in the petition, this turnabout is
realized and the theologian is allowed to live out the freedom
of thought which he enjoys as a child of God.

(2) A free theologian starts steadily and happily with the
Bible. Here must be his starting point, but not because any old
or new orthodoxy knocked it into him; it is not a law but a
privilege to start with the Bible. It is his starting point not
because he abstains from reading and appreciating other godly
and worldly books—not to forget the newspapers. He starts
with the Bible because in the Bible he learns about the free
God and free man, and as a disciple of the Bible he may himself become a witness to the divine and human freedom. He
does not start with a doctrine of the canon and of the verbal

inspiration of Holy Scripture. But he does begin, not without inspiration, with daily searching of canonical writings. They informed and still inform him. He listens to them. He studies them in many ways, not despising the analytical, the historical-critical method, in order to gain a better understanding.

There are two reasons why the analysis, including the so-called "ascertained results" of historical-critical research, or the so-called "exegetical findings," is not the starting point of a free theologian. First, these results have a tendency to change every thirty years and from one exegete to another, and are thereby disqualified as a valid starting point. Secondly, analysis of both Biblical and secular texts, even though a *conditio sine qua non* of attentive listening to their message, does in no way guarantee and presuppose this act of listening. We listen when we read and study synthetically. The free theologian combines in one single act analysis and synthesis in his reading and studies. This is meditation, the secret of which is, again, adoration. The free theologian, taking the Bible as his starting point, is led by the testimony of the Bible, or more precisely by the origin, object, and content of this testimony. Here Christ spoke to him, and he let Him speak, through the medium of this testimony. Does this imply his speaking in direct quotation and interpretation of Biblical texts and contexts? Maybe often, maybe not always. The freedom bestowed upon him by the origin, object, and content of the Biblical testimony can and must be asserted through his attempt to think and to relate in his own terms what he heard in the Bible. As an illustration I refrained in this address from using one single direct quotation from the Scriptures, with the exception of the Lord's Prayer at the beginning. It is only right to exercise this freedom earnestly and repeatedly. It is an excellent yardstick for our knowing what we say when we quote and interpret. In regard to church practice we may ask whether this attempt should not be made consistently in sermons, as contrasted to Bible study. The freedom of theology is both freedom for exegesis and freedom for what we call dogmatics. At least in his endeavor to sum up the content of a book of the Bible or even the variety of Biblical testimonies, the exegete embarks upon dogmatical thinking. Dogmatics is the conscious and systematic account of the common understanding of all Biblical testimonies with due regard for their variety. Only through a formidable misunderstanding can the two functions of theology—exegesis and dogmatics—be set one against the other.

(3) A free theologian does not deny, nor is he ashamed of, his indebtedness to a particular *philosophy* or ontology, to ways of thought and speech. These may be traditional or a bit original, old or new, coherent or incoherent. No one speaks exclusively in Biblical terms. At least the combination of these terms, if not the meaning they assume in his mind and in his mouth, are, willingly or not, of his own making. The Biblical authors themselves, incidentally, far from speaking a celestial language, spoke in many earthly languages. This is why a free theologian, who is not even a prophet or an apostle, will certainly not wish to dissociate himself from his brethren in Church and world by his claim to speak "as from heaven," "according to the gospel," or, if this is synonymous for him, "according to Luther." If he does speak with any such authority, his listeners must sense it without his explicit affirmation. To speak God's word must be an event and not the object of his assertion. Even then he speaks from within his philosophical shell, speaks in his own cumbersome vernacular which is certainly not identical with the tongues of angels, although the angels may utilize him at times. Three characteristics distinguish the free from the unfree theologian. First, he is aware of his condition. Secondly, he

stands ready to submit the coherence of his concepts and
formulations to the coherence of the divine revelation and not
conversely. Thirdly, to mention the inevitable slogan, he is
a philosopher "as though he were not," and he has his ontology "as though he had it not." A free theologian will not be
hindered by traditional conceptions from thinking and speaking in the direction from God to man, as affirmed at the outset
of this address. His ontology will be subject to criticism and
control by his theology, and not conversely. He will not
necessarily feel obligated to the philosophical *kairos*, the latest
prevailing philosophy. The gratitude of the Royal House of
Austria will, in any event, not be showered upon him. And
who knows, he may be quite glad to resort at times to an older
philosophy, like the ill-famed "Subject-Object-Scheme." If
we visualize for a moment the ideal situation of the free
theologian, we may foresee the possibility not of theology
recognizing itself in any form of philosophy, but of free
philosophy recognizing itself in free theology. Yet the free
theologian knows very well that, like a poor wretch, he does
not live in this ideal situation.

(4) A free theologian thinks and speaks within the *Church,*
within the communion of saints, whose ordinary members
happen to be not just he and his closest theological friends.
In the Church there are *confessions.* Even in the Mennonite
Church there is a confession called after the small Swiss village
of Schleitheim! Why should a free theologian not pay loving
respect to these confessions as guidance in reading, explaining,
and applying the Scriptures? True, he does not owe them the
freedom of his thought and speech. He is not bound by them.
He will listen to them very carefully. He will be free to express what they already have expressed, to express it better
if he has the talent to do so. He is equally free to acknowledge
their much better formulation of what he wants to say. He is

free, therefore, to say in his own terms what they already have said.

In the Church there are *fathers:* father Luther, father Calvin, other fathers. Why should a free theologian not be their son and disciple? But why should he insist on complete agreement with them? Why should he artificially reinterpret their findings until Luther is in agreement with him and says what he himself so badly wants to say? Why should he not respect the freedom of the fathers and let them express their wisdom and then learn from them what in his own freedom he may and can learn from them?

In the Church there are also *church governments.* Here in Germany they are even embodied in bishops. These have power to speak their mighty word through pastoral letters within the framework of their own theology which may not always be infallible. They have also power to examine, perhaps even to institute or destitute, certainly to recommend or to withhold recommendation. Why should the free theologian not at least tolerate them as they, in their mildness and prudence, as a rule tolerate him? He will certainly not become their spokesman and subordinate. Nor will he disdain the acknowledgment that a leading church figure may think and say at times the theologically right thing. He really does not —or does he?—want to get a complex, to be misled into opposition against the leadership of the Church and to feed upon his hostility until it becomes the principle of his interpretation of half, if not the whole, New Testament. More is at stake than the pro and con of the confessions, of Luther and Calvin, of the, alas, questionable church government. All this is only a sectarian pro and con. A free theologian is not a man of a sect. He thinks and he speaks his definite "Yes" or "No." He is a man of action, not of reaction. His freedom is not primarily "freedom from" but "freedom for." He bewares of becoming enmeshed in a friend-foe relationship. The free theologian loves positive tasks. The Christian community, its gathering, nurture, and mission in the world, are at stake, and the free theologian knows this. He does his research and teaching in and for the community, as one of its members entrusted with this particular task and, hopefully, with the gift to carry it through. Private Christianity is not Christianity at all. Private theology is not free theology; it is not theology at all.

(5) A free theologian works in *communication* with other theologians. He grants them the enjoyment of the same freedom with which he is entrusted. Maybe he listens to them and reads their books with only subdued joy, but at least he listens to them and reads them. He knows that the selfsame problems with which he is preoccupied may be seen and dealt with in a way different from his own. Perhaps sincerity forbids him from following or accompanying some of his fellow theologians. Perhaps he is forced to oppose and sharply contradict many, if not most, of his co-workers. He is not afraid of the *rabies theologorum*. But he refuses to part company with them, not only personally and intellectually but, above all, spiritually, just as he does not want to be dropped by them. He believes in the forgiveness of both his theological sins and theirs, if they are found guilty of some. He will not pose as the detector and judge of their sins. Not yielding one iota where he cannot responsibly do so, he continues to consider the divine and human freedom in store for them. He waits for them and asks them to wait for him. Our sadly lacking yet indispensable theological co-operation depends directly or indirectly on whether or not we are willing to wait for one another, perhaps lamenting, yet smiling with tears in our eyes. Surely in such forbearance we could dispense with the hard, bitter, and contemptuous thoughts and statements about each other, with the bittersweet book reviews and the mischievous footnotes

we throw at each other, and with whatever works of darkness there are! Is it clear in our minds that the concept of the "theological adversary" is profane and illegitimate? From my experience I would say that the Anglo-Saxon theologians, the fundamentalists probably notwithstanding, have a far better grasp of what I would like to call the "freedom of communication" than we Continentals do. They certainly do not all love each other overwhelmingly. But they treat each other as fellow creatures. We do not always act likewise. There is no ground for believing ourselves justified because of our, perhaps only illusionary, greater depth of thought.

These remarks need to be continued and drawn together systematically. Just think of the important issue of the existence and the reflection of the free theologian in his relationship to Roman Catholicism or to the prevailing political climate! Completeness, however, has not been my goal here. I merely wished to let a concrete example guide your reflection about the gift of freedom as the foundation of evangelical ethics. Therefore, I break off and close with a Biblical quotation in spite of what I said. It is an imperative, full of exegetical and other implications. Many of us are likely to have it interpreted and applied more than once with other people in mind. Today we are asked to hear it for ourselves, as theologians, hopefully as free theologians: "Finally, brethren, whatever is true, whatever is honorable, whatever is just, whatever is pure, whatever is lovely, whatever is gracious, if there is any excellence, if there is anything worthy of praise, think about these things. . . . and the peace of God will be with you."

LaVergne, TN USA
14 March 2010
175941LV00002B/2/P